Bill & Melody,

[signature]

Joshua 1:8

ANOTHER SHOT

A GAME PLAN FOR REBOUNDING IN LIFE

BY

DAVE MARTIN

emerge
publishing

TULSA, OKLAHOMA

17 16 15 14   10 9 8 7 6 5 4 3 2 1

ANOTHER SHOT — A Game Plan For Rebounding In Life

TULSA, OKLAHOMA

Published by:
Emerge Publishing, LLC
9521B Riverside Parkway, Suite 243
Tulsa, Oklahoma 74137
Phone: 888.407.4447
www.EmergePublishing.com

Cover Design: Christian Ophus | Emerge Publishing, LLC
Interior Design: Anita Stumbo

Library of Congress Cataloging-in-Publication Data

BISAC Category: SEL027000 Self Help/Success; REL012070 Christian Life

ISBN: 978-1-943127-03-0 Hardcover
ISBN: 978-1-943127-04-7 Digital

Printed in Canada.

WHAT PEOPLE ARE SAYING

The common denominator in both championship athletes and successful individuals is a coach. This is an insightful and practical book on how to rebound and be a winner in life. I highly recommend letting Dave Martin be your coach.

—GRANT HILL
NBA All-star

Every boxing champion knows the way to triumph is to take your hits and keep coming back. Life is the same ... you have to keep coming back. Dave's book Another Shot, *outlines ways to get up and go the distance. This book is the "real deal."*

—EVANDER HOLYFIELD
Five-Time Heavyweight Champion of the World

Rebounding decides the outcome of the game ... on and off the court. How badly do you want to win? Dave shares masterful insights on how to get Another Shot. When you dominate in rebounding you dominate the game!

—AMYK HUTCHENS
Speaker & Business Strategist, AmyK International, Inc.

At some time in our life, we can each relate to failure. As a basketball coach, I know this very well. Learning to bounce back is often difficult, but it is critical to success. Dave's strategies in Another Shot make it possible not only to REBOUND but WIN in life. This book transcends creed, culture and economics and is a "must read" for all leaders.

—R. Jay Barsh
Head Basketball Coach, Southeastern University

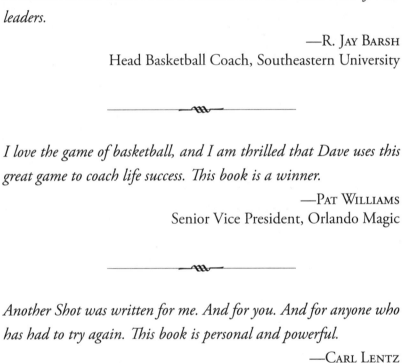

I love the game of basketball, and I am thrilled that Dave uses this great game to coach life success. This book is a winner.

—Pat Williams
Senior Vice President, Orlando Magic

Another Shot was written for me. And for you. And for anyone who has had to try again. This book is personal and powerful.

—Carl Lentz
Pastor, Hillsong New York City

I've always enjoyed Dave's work and Another Shot is right up my alley—an excellent sports metaphor for life that I grew up with! My mom, Pat Summitt, used to have her Tennessee players say

"Rebound" after every mistake so that they focused on improvement and moving forward. Another great book by an outstanding Christian, husband, father and "coach"—you will not be disappointed!

—TYLER SUMMITT
Head Coach, LA Tech Women's Basketball, Ruston, LA

Life offers us many opportunities to win or lose in whatever we are trying to achieve. The difference between winning and losing is often one inch, one second or one shot away.

It is not whether you will have a setback in your life or a horrible tragedy, it is when will this happen to you and will you be ready to rebound and go on to win the game of life.

I have had many setbacks in my life. I grew up poor. I was a poor student. I dropped out of college after two years. I was a private in the US Army. My first real job was as a waiter at a large hotel. My final job was being the senior operations executive for the Walt Disney World® Resort for ten years. Another Shot *will teach you and convince you how to get up and take another shot, no matter how many times you miss the basket during the game. The last shot often is the difference between winning and losing. Study this book to move from good to great.*

—LEE COCKERELL
Former Executive Vice President, Walt Disney World Resort
Author of *Creating Magic, The Customer Rules,
and Time Management Magic*

I absolutely love this book! My good friend, Dave Martin, inspires and gives us hope that no matter what difficulty may come into our lives, there are principles and strategies that, when applied, give us the ability to rebound in life, career, family, and finances. Using the highly competitive world of basketball, Dave talks about the desire, discipline, and determination to bounce back after life's disappointments and failures. This book is like the Old Testament leader Micah when he said, "Rejoice not against me oh my enemy, for when I fall, I shall arise!" In his encouraging, straight forward easy to read style, he shows us how we can get up, go on, and TAKE ANOTHER SHOT!

—Rob Yanok
Pastor, GraceTown Church, Columbus, Ohio
Author of *Motivations for Monday: Strategies to Jump Start your Life*

———

I personally love to watch and study successful coaches. It doesn't matter the sport. The ingredients it takes to win are universal. I also believe the principles used on the court and field can and should be used in life. This is why I've enjoyed the book "Another Shot" by Dave Martin so much. It is very effective at conveying the message of overcoming and achieving regardless of your circumstances. This book was an easy read and is loaded with useful insights. I am glad Dave wrote this. It has helped me, and I'm looking forward to getting it to as many people as possible.

—Larry Winters, Business Coach & Motivational Speaker
Founder & President of Leadership Team Development (LTD)

CONTENTS

INTRODUCTION
WHY I WROTE THIS BOOK

No one plays this game or any game perfectly.
It's the guy who recovers from his mistakes who wins.
—Phil Jackson

D O YOU KNOW of any person in any field of athletic competition who has ever achieved greatness without someone's help? Do you know of any team that has ever climbed to the pinnacle of their particular sport without the help of other people? From the NFL Super Bowl champions to the Olympic Gold Medalist in cycling, winners always have a significant, yet sometimes "invisible" person standing alongside them who trains them, teaches them, instructs them, and prepares them for the challenges they will face. This person is their coach.

But in the same way that an athlete or an athletic team can benefit from the wisdom and personal attention of a coach, all of us can benefit at times from having someone in our lives who can teach us the things we need to know while standing with us during our greatest challenges. One of my personal passions, therefore, is to help people succeed by being their "success coach" and by sharing with them the wisdom that I have gleaned and the lessons I have learned over the course of my life. In fact, I find my greatest satisfaction in helping others bypass some of the difficulties and pains that I have been forced to endure. And I am delighted whenever I can help propel someone toward greatness by giving that person the advantages of the insights I have amassed along life's way.

In many ways, being a "success coach" is not unlike being the coach of a famous athlete or a professional sports team. For instance, in both the athletic world and the personal world, people seem to need the most outside help whenever they have faced their worst defeats. In the aftermath of a great setback, a crippling disappointment, or a complete collapse, it is comforting and beneficial for a person to have a strong shoulder to lean on.

That is why I have decided to write a book about what people can do when they fail. When life knocks you down and you just don't feel like trying again, it can be easy to quit on yourself and your dreams. But the truth is, no great athlete reaches the pinnacle of success without tasting the bitter pill of defeat a few times along the way. And no championship team raises the trophy at their welcome-home parade until they flounder a few times first. So as a coach, at your lowest moment is when I want to grab you by the shoulders, make direct eye contact with you, and say, "Get back up. Get moving. You have work to do. The game is a long way from being over. Take another shot at it."

I've had my own chances to take another shot in the game of life, and my chances actually started quite early. When I was in college, for instance, I could have easily given up on myself because I was expelled for one semester. That doesn't mean I was a bad person. You don't need to start picturing me behind bars, wearing prison stripes. But I chose to attend a very strict evangelical college, where the simplest of infractions was not tolerated, and that decision often clashed with my behaviors.

In fact, an "infraction" at my college ranged from skipping classes to wearing shoes without socks, so those of you who attended a public university would probably not understand the stern mindset that governed the college I attended. However, on this particular occasion, I readily admitted my willful violation of the rules, and, as a result, my school determined that my friend and I would not be welcome there for the duration of that semester or the next one.

When this had happened to other students in the past, those students had usually chosen either to quit college altogether or to enroll at another school, thus avoiding the embarrassment of returning to the scene of their humiliation. But I decided to reject both of these popular options. Instead, I wanted another shot at earning my degree. I wanted to prove to myself and others that, although I had experienced a setback, I was still in the game. I was not beaten.

So I took the required time away; then I returned to school to finish my education. But oddly, what stands out most to me about that experience is not the memory of my misdeed or the disgrace of my expulsion. My most significant memory is the encouragement I received from my professors, my friends, and even the president of the college for being willing to come back and finish the race. They expressed admiration for my tenacity and my determination. As a result, I learned a valuable lesson that has helped shape my life since then: People of character focus on the end result. Failure, setbacks, and disappointments are only final if we fail to get back on our feet and try again.

So after I started coaching other people to triumph in the game of life, I made this theme one of the central themes in my message to them: You will never lose if you get back up. You may need to make adjustments along the way, and you may need to realign yourself with the truth sometimes. You may even need a complete overhaul from time to time or a new approach to your dreams and goals. But you must always come back. You must always try again. You must always take another shot.

I love the game of basketball, and, as a "coach" in my own right, I see a whole lot of parallels between this truth that I teach to my students and the fundamentals that guide the game of "hoops." In basketball, for instance, the rebounder is the designated team member who is responsible for grabbing the ball after a missed shot so another shot can be attempted. What a great analogy for life. Like a rebounder, we must be the one to grab the loose ball and put it back up again in an extra effort to score.

For the next several chapters, therefore, I want to act as your coach while I use the analogy of the game of basketball (and sports in general) to give you some instruction about life that can help you get back up, get back in the game, and get your hands on the ball one more time so you can take another shot and finally score. I want to share with you my experiences and impart to you the things I have learned so you won't be tempted to throw in the towel and surrender to the obstacles that stand between you and your goals, between you and the success you seek.

Coaching is not always an easy job, because athletes don't always enjoy hearing what their coaches have to say. For that reason, some of the lessons I will be teaching and some of the points I will be making in this book may be uncomfortable for you. But the goal here is not your comfort; the goal is your success. Teams do not win championships by taking the easy road or by doing only what the players feel like doing at the time. They win by being determined and by showing a willingness to do those things that seem impossible when they first consider them. They win by listening, by learning, and by being committed to hard work. You must be willing to listen and learn, too.

So I hope this book will inspire you. I hope it will motivate you. And I hope you will find enough wisdom here to stir thoughts and ideas that you can jot down for your future consideration and use. I hope you will take away what speaks to you and keep this book in your library for frequent future reference. But most of all, I hope you will find answers and truths in this book that will change your life. And I hope that these truths speak so powerfully to you that, whenever you find yourself knocked down on the canvas, you will pick this book up again, read it through to refresh your memory, and then get back in the game where you belong. It's just what winners do.

POUNDING THE BOARDS

The real glory is being knocked to your knees and then coming back. That's real glory. That's the essence of it.

—Vince Lombardi

WHAT DO THE following people have in common: Wilt Chamberlain, Kareem Abdul-Jabbar, Moses Malone, Dennis Rodman? A few years ago, I asked this question at a conference in Hawaii, and the people in the audience yelled, "Basketball!" That's true! All these men were certainly great basketball players.

But that's not the connecting thread I was looking for, so I asked again, "What do all these *basketball players* have in common?" And the people there said, "Tall!" They knew that all these guys were extremely tall.

Again, true! But that still wasn't the shared trait that I wanted them to notice, so I asked one more time, "What do all these *tall basketball players* have in common?"

"They're all retired," somebody shouted. And that's true, too. But that still wasn't the answer I was looking for. So at that point, I decided to answer my own question.

Sure, these guys are tall, and all of them are basketball players. All of them are retired, and all of them were top-notch competitors in their heyday. All of them are African-American, and all of them are rich. But the common trait I wanted my audience to see was that all of these men were great rebounders. All of them played "center" for their respective teams, because they were the best at pounding the boards and pulling down rebounds.

In fact, Wilt Chamberlain was the greatest rebounder of all time, accumulating a career total of 23,924 rebounds. Kareem Abdul-Jabbar was third all-time with 17,440. Moses Malone was fifth with 16,212. And Dennis Rodman was twenty-second on the list of all-time rebounders.

I don't know if you are a basketball fan or if you follow sports at all. But even if you don't keep track of the Los Angeles Lakers or the Chicago Bulls, you recognize the names of these basketball "greats." And you recognize their names because these men were renowned for their exploits. They were famous, and they eventually became pop cultural icons who were recognizable even when they weren't suited up for a ballgame.

I live in Orlando, Florida, the home of the Orlando Magic, so I am quite familiar with some of these guys myself. I am also familiar with the great rebounders who have played for my home team. For four years, Shaquille O'Neal played for the Magic (fourteenth on the all-time list of career rebounders). And in more recent years, Orlando was the home of Dwight Howard. These guys are famous too, just like Chamberlain, Rodman, and Malone. And they are well known for the same reason: They were great rebounders who were paid millions of dollars each year for the specific purpose of snatching rebounds off the backboard. In fact, Dwight Howard is still a great player, finishing fourth in rebounding this past season as a member of the Houston Rockets.

But what is it, you may ask, that makes a rebounder such an important player, commanding a multimillion-dollar salary in exchange for his cherished talent? Why is this one position so extremely vital to the owners and managers of a professional basketball team? It's because a great rebounder gives his team a second chance to score. Rebounding creates the opportunity for another shot. Simply put, rebounding is the art of successfully gaining possession of the basketball after a missed or failed attempt. It is the act of correcting a mistake so the end result turns out well. It is an effort to turn a failure into a success. It's a "do-over," a "mulligan." And that is what we all need sometimes— the opportunity to try again, to have one more chance, to take another shot at the goal.

A GAME OF UNLIMITED CHANCES

No doubt you have watched enough basketball in your lifetime to know that the players miss a lot of shots. Even the best players, when they are being aggressively defended, fail to score about 50 percent of the time. So the center, usually the tallest player on the team, is assigned the responsibility of going after those missed shots so his team can retain possession of the ball and have another opportunity to score.

All my life, I have been struck by the countless similarities between sports and life. Both sports and life require know-how, both demand talent and skill, and both can lead to glorious and fulfilling victories. But both are marked with obstacles and set-backs too, with mistakes and with crushing defeats. Both are marked with opposition, competition, and failure. And both offer us challenges, as well as opportunities to correct our mistakes and to rise above our failures. In athletic competition, there is always the next game or the next season. In a basketball game, there is always the chance to rebound a missed shot. And in life, we must create the same opportunities to turn failures into successes.

Have you ever had a failed attempt or a significant setback in your life? Most of us have. In 1921, at the age of 39, former state senator and assistant secretary of the Navy, Franklin D. Roosevelt, was struck with polio, completely losing the use of both of his legs. But rather than allowing the event to define him for the rest of his life, Roosevelt returned to politics three years later and was elected governor of New York in 1928. Then, although mostly confined to a wheelchair, he became president of the United States at the age of 50. FDR did not allow his fate to become his future. He rebounded, took another shot, was known for his optimism, and led the nation triumphantly through both the Great Depression and World War II.

The Bible is filled with stories about people who failed and had setbacks in life, too, people who were knocked down by the things they did not see coming or the things they were unprepared to handle. And the Bible never glosses over these losses. Instead, it shows us in brutal detail the pain, the anguish, and the humiliation that marked the failures of people we now know as the great warriors and icons of the faith. But then it presents the beautiful and encouraging picture of how these people rebounded and how they rose from the ashes.

Remember Moses? He murdered an Egyptian, yet God chose him to lead the Israelite nation out of captivity. He made excuses to God, claiming that he was not a suitable spokesman for the Jewish people. But God set those excuses aside and gave Moses a mouthpiece in his brother, Aaron. Moses also had an anger problem, becoming irate at the nation and disobeying God by striking the rock in order to produce a miraculous flow of water for the people. Yet in spite of these things, God used Moses time and time again, speaking to him face to face "as a man speaks to his friend" (Exodus 33:11, ESV).

Remember Peter? Peter was one of the three apostles who were closest to Jesus, and he swore that he would stand by the Lord no matter what happened. Then, before the sun could rise the morning after that bold declaration, Peter denied even knowing Jesus, cursing his very name to a little servant girl. Yet

Peter was reunited, restored, and recharged, and he became the foundation of the early church.

Remember Jacob? Remember David? Remember Paul? All these great men had setbacks. They all had failures. But they all rebounded, and we know them for their successes, not their failures. We know them for their life's work and for their faith.

At some point, all of us have tried and failed. We have gone for broke and become broke. We have played the game and lost. Yet we are not finished. Not at all! We will get back up, get back in, and get back to work.

But to drive home this point, let's get back to our sports analogy, because life is exactly like a basketball game. When we fail, we always have the opportunity to regain possession of the ball and to correct our mistakes. We have the opportunity to turn a loss into a gain, a defeat into a victory. And there is no limit to how many times we can try. But in order to have repeated opportunities to pluck victory from the jaws of defeat, we have to be able to rebound the basketball.

TRAITS OF A GOOD REBOUNDER

There are several attributes that all good rebounders possess. Whether we are talking about the game of basketball or the game of life, rebounding is definitely an acquired skill. Sure, the players who are the best rebounders on the court are players who have the natural abilities they need to perform the job. All of them are seven feet tall or close to it. All of them are big and strong. All of them are quick, and they can jump. But these are physical attributes, not skills. I am much more fascinated by the "art" of rebounding. I am more intrigued by the abilities that must be learned and honed over the course of many years and through a lot of active participation in the game itself, because I believe that when we look closely at what it takes to be a successful rebounder on the basketball court, we will find the keys to what it takes to successfully rebound in life.

There are specific attributes, techniques, attitudes, and qualities that an individual must have in order to successfully rebound the ball and take another shot. And the traits I want to highlight are the ones obtained through experience and hard work, because these are the traits that distinguish the great players from the average ones. And these are the qualities that distinguish great people from the common ones. Great people bounce back. They rebound. But they rebound because they have developed and nurtured the specific skills they need to deal with life's setbacks and to turn life's missed opportunities into second chances to score.

Coach Don Meyer, the respected men's college basketball coach who accumulated more than 900 career wins prior to his death in 2014, was noted for saying, "Complacency is the forerunner of mediocrity. You can never work too hard on attitude, effort, and technique."

In the pages that follow, therefore, I want to use these three areas of focus—attitude, effort, and technique—as a framework for sharing with you the valuable lessons I see in the intersection of life and sports. We will start by looking closely at the three attitudes that are critical for a frontrunner to possess: determination, aggressiveness, and fearlessness. Then we will examine another three areas where your efforts must be concentrated if you want to become the best player on the court and in life: preparation, positioning, and teamwork. And finally, we will use the remaining chapters for a detailed look at five techniques that are the result of work and hard practice, techniques that are essential for a winning performance on the basketball court and in the real world: strength, balance, contact, timing, and control.

I want this to be your comeback book. Previous failures and missed shots are in the past. So use the coaching techniques within these pages to change your thinking, to adjust your positioning, to assess your competition, to redraw your game plan, and to take another shot at victory, because victory comes not to those who are perfect, but to those who persist and to those who make corrections as the game unfolds. Victory comes to those who continue to do what they do until they finally get it right. And the trophy is eventually raised by the one who can finally take possession of that elusive bouncing ball and take one more shot at his goals.

ATTITUDE

THE ATTRIBUTES OF A WINNER

DETERMINATION

The power to win must come from within.

—Anonymous

S OME PEOPLE "think" they can; other people "believe" they can. But great rebounders "know" they can rebound the basketball. There's no hoping or believing to it. In fact, the unspoken motto of a Hall of Fame rebounder is, "The ball belongs to me."

So confidence is an essential trait of a good rebounder, whether on the basketball court or in life. But determination is the core attribute that breeds this kind of confidence and the fundamental characteristic that produces results. For this reason, determination is the quality you need most in order to bounce back from your past failures or from the missteps that have taken you further from your goals.

In America, we absolutely love determined people. There's just something about the American mindset that applauds the individual who refuses to accept defeat, who won't give up, and who won't go away. Whenever Rocky is knocked to the canvas, we groan with agony, but we cheer when he gets back up. And our adrenalin soars when he lands a solid punch of his own. Whenever the little guy gets sand kicked in his face, we feel his pain, but then our emotions surge when he finally takes a stand and defends himself. And whenever the Terminator says, "I'll be back," we feel like rolling up our sleeves and helping him in his crusade.

PERSISTENCE WILL PREVAIL

The typical American understands determination, and we delight in seeing an individual or a team rise from obscurity to national prominence through hard work, grit, and guts. This is one reason sports are so popular in this country. We revel in watching the little guy overcome incredible odds to defeat invincible foes. We are thrilled whenever the "hero" prevails under seemingly impossible circumstances to achieve totally unexpected results. In family rooms, friends' homes, and sports bars across the country, we jump up, cheering madly whenever a display of raw determination propels the underdog to victory, yelling to anyone who will listen, "Did you *see* that?"

Determination is perhaps the most important trait that separates those who just get by from those who are truly remarkable. It is the difference between Hall of Famers and benchwarmers. Most people achieve their limited success by the sheer force of their talent and charm. But the truly great performers in sports and in life rise to a higher level than their peers by developing a determined attitude regarding their goals. They refuse to retreat in the face of setbacks. They do not dodge disappointments. They don't quiver in the presence of opposition. And they never back down from the possibility of risk. In fact, men and women with determination seem to move forward in spite of these things, because people of purpose are willing to do whatever it takes to get back on their feet and to reclaim possession of their own lives whenever a problem has knocked them to the floor or an opportunity has slipped through their fingers.

But while we are contemplating the undeniable importance of determination, we need to realize that determination has a cousin. And this cousin's name is persistence. Although there is a great family resemblance between determination and persistence, there also is an important distinction. The two are not the same.

Determination is the willingness to give it all you've got. It is the intention to let nothing stand in your way. It is an attitude that you are not going to be defeated or let yourself lose. A person with determination will do whatever it takes to overcome the obstacles in his path and to rise above his challenges.

Persistence, however, has more to do with longevity. It is the quality that causes a person to claim his turf and refuse to go away. The person with persistence is determined, for sure, but he also is resilient. He simply will not walk away, and he cannot accept defeat as his final verdict. He is never a quitter. He remains steadfast.

When speaking of this vital quality of determination and of the accompanying quality of persistence, Calvin Coolidge, the thirtieth president of the United States, once said, "Nothing in the world can take the place of persistence. Talent will not; nothing is more common than unsuccessful men with talent. Genius will not; unrewarded genius is almost a proverb. Education will not; the world is full of educated derelicts. Persistence and determination alone are omnipotent. The slogan 'Press On' has solved and always will solve the problems of the human race."

So the determined man refuses to back down from a fight while the persistent man refuses to quit until the fight is over. And thus, determination and persistence are the traits that cause a man to rise again, to claim his stake, and to refuse to be moved. They are the complementary qualities that won't allow a person with greatness in his soul to accept defeat as his final verdict in anything he attempts to do.

On a freezing February morning in 1916, seven-year-old Glenn Cunningham and his older brother, Floyd, left their small Kansas home to walk to school. It was a bitterly cold day, and one of the boys' chores that morning was to start a fire in the potbelly stove at the schoolhouse so the classroom would be warm when the other students arrived.

On this morning, like all the mornings that preceded it,

everything went according to plan as they poured the fuel onto the firewood inside the stove. But when they lit the fire, the stove suddenly exploded and flames instantly engulfed the one-room schoolhouse. Apparently, someone had filled the fuel can with gasoline rather than kerosene, and the resulting fire killed Floyd, leaving Glenn barely clinging to life.

As he lay in his hospital bed following this tragic accident, Glenn heard the doctors tell his mother that he would probably not survive his wounds. He was just too badly burned to pull through his ordeal. Nevertheless the resolute seven-year-old found the will to live, and he slowly began to improve. But after a few more days had passed, Glenn once again overheard the doctors tell his mother that they would have to amputate his legs, because his legs had been so severely burned they would be useless to Glenn except as a source of infection and constant pain.

Yet in spite of his agony, Glenn didn't want his legs removed. So Glenn's mother, mindful that her son had already lost his brother, refused to let the doctors take his legs too. And lying in that hospital bed for two weeks with his lifeless lower body wrapped in bandages, Glenn made up his mind that he was somehow going to walk again.

For a while the doctors' pessimistic prognosis seemed to be more reliable than Glenn's lofty goals. When Glenn finally went home and his bandages were removed, he realized that he had lost all the toes on his left foot, and the transverse arch on his right foot was severely damaged. In addition, the flesh on his knees and shins had been eaten away by the flames. And Glenn's right leg was grossly misshapen, fully two inches shorter than his left leg.

So at home Glenn's parents would spend hours each day massaging their son's legs, trying to keep them from becoming too stiff to bend. And Glenn's mother often pushed her son's wheelchair outside in the sunlight so Glenn could get some fresh air while allowing the heat of the sun to warm his damaged muscles.

Then one day in 1919, Mrs. Cunningham looked out the window and saw her son lift himself out of his wheelchair and throw himself onto the ground. Using his arms, he dragged his body along the ground to the picket fence surrounding their yard, and slowly, painfully, he pulled himself upright so he could lean on the fence while trying to walk. Astonished by the scene that was unfolding before her, Glenn's mother rushed to her son's aid. But Glenn refused to accept her help. In spite of his pain, he was determined to force his legs to work.

So each day after that, Glenn would return to the fence, using the sturdy wood to support himself as he tried to learn to stand on his feet and to move himself around the yard. Through sheer determination and persistence, he continued the agonizing process until he became better and better at balancing himself and using his legs to walk. And as the days passed, he wore a noticeable path along the entire length of that white picket fence.

When Glenn finally felt like he had mastered the process of walking, he started running, and he discovered that his legs didn't hurt while he was running. So to the amazement of his doctors, Glenn started running everywhere he went. In fact, the people in Glenn's hometown came to know him as "the boy who runs," and by the time he was twelve years old, Glenn could out-run any kid at his school. So he joined the school's track team, and his running became legendary.

In fact, in high school, Glenn became a miler and set a national record in his event. Then he attended the University of Kansas, excelling academically and as a valued member of the track team there, setting a new NCAA record for the mile and being honored as the 1933 recipient of the nation's highest award for an amateur athlete.

Eventually, Glenn became known as the "Kansas Flyer," and in both 1932 and 1936, he was selected to represent the United States in the Olympics. But in 1934, eighteen years after hearing doctors say that he would never walk again, Glenn Cunningham, considered by many to be the greatest American miler of all time, ran into history in Madison Square Garden by breaking the world record for the fastest indoor mile.

The person who prevails is the person who refuses to give up. Life is a struggle just as athletic competition is a struggle. But in every battle, your mental outlook will be the key to your success or your key to failure. The person with mental toughness, with resolve and willpower, is the person who will triumph. That person will be a good rebounder. And it is necessary to be a good rebounder, no matter what your goals may be, because you will never hit all your shots all the time. Quite often, the ball will fall short, float long, or veer to the right or the left. Other people or circumstances will interfere with your attempts to score, and you will be thrown off stride. So when the ball fails to go through the hoop, it becomes necessary to regroup and to try again. But to try again, you have to get the ball back, and that's when determination becomes key.

AS MANY TIMES AS IT TAKES

In life, as in basketball, nobody is going to just hand you the ball. Nobody is going to feel sorry for you and give you an unobstructed path to the goal. When there's a loose ball, everybody will be going after it. Everybody will be trying to establish position, and you are definitely going to feel the pushback that comes from the competition. But even if you manage to overcome those who stand in the way of your ambitions, the ball itself is going to present you with some challenges. It will bounce around and respond to every touch and to every impact it makes with the rim, the backboard, the players, and the floor. Quite often, the ball will slip through your fingers while you are desperately trying to grab it. It will evade you by bouncing just beyond your reach.

Think about it! How many times has success evaded you in the slightest ways? How many times has it slipped through your fingers just when you thought you had it in your grasp? How many times have unforeseen circumstances knocked you out of position just when you believed you had things under control? How many times have your dreams come so close only to bounce off your fingertips?

Both the successful rebounder and the successful individual

are people who don't give up easily. Both know that success is not a one-step process. Success is a series of wise decisions and calculated actions that are designed to lead to an ultimate goal. Every decision requires focus, and every action requires the best that one can give. To ignore or minimize the little things that comprise one's life is to settle eventually for mediocrity rather than greatness and to accept the commonplace rather than the exceptional. So the people who manage to bounce back from the inevitable missteps along their journey are those people who are determined to do all the little things right every single time. They fix issues and resolve problems as soon as those problems become apparent. They never let any little piece of their lives be less than exactly right. They continue to move forward toward their goals, and they do so with an intentional pursuit of excellence.

There's an old Japanese proverb that says, "Fall down seven times, get up eight." And the Bible declares, "For though a righteous man falls seven times, he rises again" (Proverbs 24:16, NIV). So don't quit. Never quit. God knows you will fall down once in a while and you will occasionally miss some shots. Your life will not be a flawless performance. But the key to long-term success is to keep getting back on your feet. So keep trying to retrieve the ball after you've missed one of your attempts at the goal. And when you do that, you will be amazed how far you can go. As seven-time NBA rebounding champion Dennis Rodman once said, "The one thing that I do that nobody else does is jump three and four times for one rebound. I'm hungrier than those other guys out there."

A successful rebounder is not the kind of person who will make one attempt to regain the basketball and then walk away. You won't hear him say, "Well, I missed it this time. Maybe next time." The successful rebounder is determined to get the ball back, and he won't give up until he does. He will try again and again to get position on his opponent, to jump higher than his opponent, and to pursue the loose ball with more aggressiveness than his opponent. And if he fails in his attempt to retrieve the ball, he will try to steal it from the one who does eventually take control of it. He will never simply surrender to "fate" or submit to circumstances or to someone else's efforts to take possession of the basketball. He will keep going after that ball as many times as it takes.

ADVICE FROM YOUR SUCCESS COACH

Do you need to become more determined? Do you need to develop more tenacity? Do you need more resolve in your life? My coaching advice to you is this:

1. Write down your goals. Put into words exactly what you want to accomplish.

2. Place your written goals where you can see them and read them every morning and every night.

3. Determine that you will undertake at least one action every day to propel yourself toward your goals. Some days, you may do something small. Other days, your steps forward will be more significant. But every effort,

no matter how slight, will have the effect of moving you closer to your goals. So do it. Every! Single! Day!

4. And never, ever give up. Never quit.

The key to your long-term success will be your capacity to persist in the face of setbacks and disappointments. You must resolve to be, therefore, not a perfect shooter, but a tenacious rebounder. And this determination or lack of determination will ultimately determine the outcome of your life, the condition of your relationships, and the storyline of all your pursuits, whether those pursuits are personal or professional.

Success is a series of tiny achievements reached by an unwillingness to back down. Success is the ability to snap back, to rebound, and to get back up after being knocked down. It's a steadfast resolve and a persistent stubbornness that few people can understand. So make up your mind to stay in the fight for the long haul, and make up your mind to stay in the fight until you win.

Our libraries are full of stories of everyday men and women who became great and who left their permanent mark on the world due, not to their talents or wisdom or wealth or connections, but rather to their sheer determination to prevail and their sheer persistence in life. Without exception, all these great people had at least one or two failures somewhere along the way. Yet they saw their failures as a launching pad to a better future, not as a pitiful conclusion to their dreams.

We often hear stories like the one about Glenn Cunningham,

and we are intrigued by the persistence of other people. But deep down inside, we wonder, "Could I have done that? Under the same circumstances, would I have kept going? Do I have that same level of determination? Do I have what it takes?"

Somewhere in your house, I bet you have a can of WD-40 that you use when you are making repairs and doing chores. But have you ever considered the story behind that little can of WD-40? The fact is, there's a story of determination behind almost everything in life that we take for granted.

WD-40 literally stands for Water Displacement, 40th attempt. That's the name straight out of the lab book used by the chemist who created WD-40 back in 1953. The chemist, Norm Larsen, was attempting to concoct a formula to prevent corrosion, a goal that is achieved by displacing water. And Norm's persistence eventually paid off when he finally perfected his formula on the 40th try.

If at first you don't succeed, you're pretty normal, because rarely does a great person achieve greatness on his first try. If at first you don't succeed, then you definitely qualify for membership among the ranks of the world's most accomplished people, because accomplished people gained their knowledge and wisdom through successive failures. So hang in there, and refuse to walk away from your dreams. Become a great rebounder by showing determination and persistence. After all, the next shot you take could be the greatest shot of your life. But you can't score if you don't shoot. And you can't shoot if you don't rebound from your past misses. And you can't rebound if you quit too soon. So learn to bounce back, and become a champion who exceeds all expectations.

Perhaps Tommy Lasorda, the manager of the Los Angeles Dodgers for twenty years, said it best, "The difference between the impossible and the possible lies in a man's determination." Determination is definitely the pathway to victory.

AGGRESSIVENESS

Timid athletes wait for opportunities;
aggressive athletes make them.

—Anonymous

E VERY TEAM wants the playmaker. The playmaker can turn
the game around in seconds. The playmaker can right
the ship. The playmaker, through determination and
talent, can take complete control of the basketball court. The
playmaker can make you believe again.

But what makes a person a "playmaker"? What gives an athlete that "edge" that somehow compels him to take control of
the game when nobody else seems able to and then to do what
mere mortals can't do in order to snatch victory from the jaws
of defeat?

THE BUCK STOPS HERE

First and foremost, a playmaker is given to consistent, aggressive play. He is always part of the action, and he never thinks that it is acceptable to admit defeat or to let somebody else take the bull by the horns when he knows that he can. So the playmaker—the one who commands multimillion-dollar contracts and multiple endorsement deals—the one whose jersey is being sold in every department store from Seattle to Key West—is the one who is hungry to willingly take responsibility for the game and forcefully rewrite the outcome of the game to suit his own interests in winning.

There is no sport where a person can make a claim to greatness without being aggressive. Sports are competitive, and a winner has to strive, to stretch, and to excel against stiff competition in order to triumph. It's just the nature of athletic competition. Watch a tennis match, for instance, or a football game, a track event, or a basketball game, and you will quickly see that the person who claims the prize is the person who is aggressive in his pursuit of every point, every advantage, and every loose ball.

Each sport is a little different. The rules are different, the scoring is different, and the skills required for the game are different. But the goal is always the same: to win. And winning is achieved through no-holds-barred, take no prisoners, win at all costs, heart-pounding, bloodletting play. In sports, the feeble need not apply. And in life, the weak and timid also get left in the dust.

So you have to make a decision to be aggressive in life, not toward people, because people are not your enemies. Many professional athletes who compete aggressively with one another on the field of play are good friends when they're not in the throes of battle. But you have to learn to be aggressive in the pursuit of your goals. You have to learn to be aggressive in your struggle against the delays, setbacks, missteps, temporary failures, and changes in the environment that make you want to throw up your hands and quit. You have to be aggressive toward your own tendency to put only half your heart into the pursuit and only half your energy into the fight.

Aggressiveness is an attitude. It is the mental state of knowing that, in order to win, you must be assertive, forceful, and fierce. But how does this kind of mental attitude translate into everyday life? How can we live aggressively and yet stay out of jail? What does an aggressive life look like for the person who wants to win, but who wants to be respected and admired at the same time?

Aggressiveness in sports, as in life, is a positive thing, not a negative thing. It is a good thing, not something bad like physical aggression or aggressive driving. So my coaching advice to you is to understand that the kind of aggressiveness that is healthy and that precedes both personal and professional success is the kind of aggressiveness that motivates us to do three things. First, it motivates us to take the initiative. Second, it motivates us to work hard. And third, it motivates us to withstand the bumps and the bruises that are part of the struggle to prevail.

So first and foremost, aggressiveness motivates us to take the initiative. For years, coaches have told their athletes, "You will never become a ballplayer by walking after the ball." How true! You have to run. You have to get up and get in the game of life. Stop sitting on the sidelines, watching others do what you know you could do and do better. Get started. This is life coaching rule number one: Be a participant in life.

You've probably heard the saying, "God gives every bird its food, but he does not throw it into its nest" (J.G. Holland). In a similar way, God has given you gifts, talents, opportunities, and resources. But it's time for you to get busy using those things to your advantage and the advantage of others. God isn't going to make you move your feet to go somewhere new or open your mouth to say something important. You have to do those things for yourself.

If you have enough initiative in your life to read this book, then you have a great idea inside you that you have put off for years. So sit down today with a blank piece of paper, and write down everything you can think of that relates to your idea. What do you need to get started? Who will you enlist to help you build your dream? What is a workable timeline for making this thing happen? What should be done first? What can you do today, this week, and this month to move your idea forward?

So you've had a few setbacks! Everyone has. But I recently found this list while doing some research and was amazed at the obstacles these people overcame:

- Booker T. Washington was born into slavery.
- Thomas Edison was deaf.

- Abraham Lincoln was born to illiterate parents.
- Lord Byron had a club foot.
- Robert Louis Stevenson had tuberculosis.
- Alexander Pope had a hunchback.
- Admiral Nelson had only one eye.
- Julius Caesar had epilepsy.
- Henry Ford and Walt Disney both filed for bankruptcy.
- Frank Sinatra suffered with bipolar disorder.

Yet these men, in spite of their handicaps, made history. Then there was Louis Pasteur, so nearsighted that he had a difficult time finding his way around in his own laboratory without glasses. And there was Helen Keller, who could not see or hear, but who graduated from Radcliffe College, becoming the first deaf and blind person to receive a bachelor's degree. So let go of your past missteps, mistakes, and failures, and begin anew. Aggressively take the initiative to step in and step up. Don't just be there; be *all* there. Don't just watch; participate. Don't just wish; do.

God has gifted each of us with amazing creativity. Perhaps you are most creative at problem solving. Maybe you are really good at putting together a budget. Could be you are great at communicating with a group, holding the attention of children, or organizing an event. Don't try to copy others or to follow them completely. And don't let envy cause you to idolize others while underestimating your own potential. Use your own innate creativity to become a playmaker. Be the one who jumps in, turns the ship, and changes the game. There's no better time to get started than now. So do it.

HARD WORK IS HAPPY WORK

This brings me to the second way we need to be aggressive in life: We need to work. Work hard. Goals worth having will only be met through hard work. So greet each day with the expectation of working hard, and greet each day with the expectation of achieving results because of your determined, assertive, uncompromising effort—your sweat equity, as they say. Zig Ziglar, one of the best-known writers and inspirational speakers of all time, said, "Success is dependent upon the glands—sweat glands."

So hard work is the basis for everything that is worth having in life. It is the basis of a good marriage, the basis of a healthy family, the basis of a strong spiritual life, and the basis for professional success. Hard work is the first step toward any meaningful achievement. Like the farmer who must plant his seeds before he can harvest his crops, a person must be willing to pay the price in personal sacrifice and hard work before he can bask in the accomplishment of his goals. In fact, nothing will bring you to the attention of others faster and in a more positive way than developing a reputation as a hard worker. Those who are in a position to promote you are always looking for individuals with a strong work ethic, and they are always genuinely impressed when they finally find a person like that, because a strong work ethic coupled with reliable character is genuinely rare.

Today, many Americans fail to work hard because many Americans are dissatisfied with their jobs. Under the headline, "Recent Gallup poll reveals that few Americans actually like their jobs," Nicole Elliott wrote in June 2013 for *The Celebrity Café*, "A recent Gallup poll reveals that only 30 percent of Americans are actively engaged in their jobs. Gallup interviewed 150,000 full-time and part-time workers for their State of the American Workplace report. Twenty percent of workers report that they hate going to work and 50 percent report a persistent case of Monday blues."

"Why are these statistics so important?" Elliott asks.

"(Disengaged employees) are more likely than engaged employees to steal from their companies, negatively influence their coworkers, miss workdays, and drive customers away," she explains, quoting from *The Gallup Blog*.

Amazingly, the apostle Paul addressed this same issue some 2,000 years ago in the Bible when he wrote a letter to his protégé, Titus. But while Elliott was reporting recent findings about modern American workers, Paul was directing Titus to pass along life-coaching advice to some first-century slaves, people who had a lot less reason to be satisfied with their "jobs."

In his letter to Titus, Paul said, "Teach slaves to be subject to their masters in everything, to try to please them, not to talk back to them, and not to steal from them, but to show that they can be fully trusted, so that in every way they will make the teaching about God our Savior attractive" (Titus 2:9-10, NIV). Paul wanted even the slaves of his day to understand that work

45

conduct and productivity are reflections of Christian character. Christians should be the hardest workers and the most diligent employees, and they should have the most productive days, because people notice.

In the Bible, Solomon also had something to say about this subject. He asked, "Do you see someone skilled in their work? They will serve before kings; they will not serve before officials of low rank" (Proverbs 22:29, NIV). So success is the product of aggressiveness, and promotion is the product of hard work. Advancement is the product of diligence, and prosperity is the product of tenacity. As Gary Player once noted, isn't it amazing that "the harder you work, the luckier you get?"

Both common sense and experience teach us that a person's willingness to work hard can open doors of opportunity for him. The basketball player who is willing to work just a little harder than his teammates is the player who will eventually pull down more rebounds and lead his team to victory. And the person who is willing to go just a little farther, push just a little harder, and show just a little more determination and aggressiveness in his pursuit of excellence is the person who will eventually succeed.

But this kind of mentality takes true commitment and effort. It also takes real patience and determination. Perhaps Magic Johnson, the great basketball player and rebounder for the Los Angeles Lakers, said it best: "Talent is never enough. With few exceptions, the best players are the hardest workers."

So learn to work, and develop a strong work ethic. But if you intend to have an admirable work ethic, then actually work while you're working. Don't just *plan* to work, and don't just *talk* about how much you work. Work.

There's a new term that has emerged in recent years in the field of business psychology. The term is "AWP" (Absent While Present). And we see this phenomenon all around us in the American workplace.

The sign in the store window read NO HELP WANTED. As two men passed by, one said to the other, "You should apply; you'd be great." And the thought of that scene is funny to us because too many people are just like this guy. Too many people get up in the mornings, shower and shave, eat breakfast, drive to the office, and punch the clock, thinking they are working. In fact, if you were to call them at the office, they would tell you that they are "working." But in reality, they hardly work at all. They spend most of their time on Facebook or Twitter or talking to their friends or checking their account balances on their cell phones.

If you intend to have a believable work ethic, then you need to actually *work* while you're at work. You need to do some work while you're collecting a salary for working. You need to do more than just show up; you need to participate. Actually, you need to do more than participate; you need to aggressively push things forward. You need to be out front, taking the lead, driving the operation, kicking butt and taking no prisoners. You need to do this on the job, you need to do this on the basketball court, and you need to do this in life. Nothing of real substance comes to the half-hearted or to those semi-committed people who seem to be entrenched in office cubicles throughout America. The ball goes to the person who aggressively goes after it and refuses to surrender it, and success goes to the person who aggressively goes after it and refuses to surrender it to circumstances, problems, difficulties, or setbacks. Achievement goes to the person who refuses to lose.

That's why the victor's crown usually goes not to the team with the greatest reputation or to the athlete with the biggest contract, but rather to the athlete and the team who are willing to put in the hard work that is necessary to qualify for the title of "champion."

TROUBLE IS A FRIEND

The third coaching lesson that I want to share with you regarding the role of aggressiveness in a person's success is that aggressiveness, though necessary, can sometimes have one bad side effect. When we become assertive and take the initiative, we can often get a lot of bumps and bruises as a result of our assertiveness.

Consider basketball. The competition is intense. The fast guys drive, and the big guys jump high above the rim. It can get really rough down there under the basket. The physical contact is terrible, and basketball players wear no protective gear. So quite often, you will see basketball players limping off the court with sprained ankles or being carried off the court with broken bones or torn ligaments.

Think of the rebounder, for instance. When he jostles for position to retrieve the missed shot, he is quite likely to catch an elbow to the face or a shoulder to the jaw. To come out with the ball means that he will probably come out with some "war wounds" too. Yet he is willing to accept the bumps and the bruises as the price he must pay for the satisfaction of getting the ball back so his team can take another shot.

And this is the way it is in life. As you engage the competition, you will get knocked around a bit, bruised, and beat up. You will suffer some predictable setbacks—perhaps in your finances, perhaps in some unwanted changes affecting your relationships, or possibly in some other area of life that will leave you damaged in some way. So be prepared. Be forewarned. Pain is part of the "game." But keep your eyes on the prize.

Muhammad Ali was undoubtedly one of the most successful athletes in history. His feats are globally acclaimed and universally applauded. But Ali knew something about the bumps and bruises associated with his sport, both the physical bumps and the emotional ones. Ali also knew something about bouncing back. He knew something about rebounding. Not only was he forced during his career to rebound from some terrible defeats, he also was forced to rebound from a four-year suspension from the sport. After reaching the pinnacle of the boxing world, he basically had to start from scratch and claw his way back to the top, a journey that took seven additional years of his life. Like so many high achievers, however, Ali knew what it took to get to the top and to stay there.

Ali once said, "The fight is won or lost far away from witnesses—behind the lines, in the gym, and out there on the road, long before I dance under those lights." In other words, victory doesn't necessarily come to the fastest or the smartest or the biggest or the tallest. Victory comes to the person who pays the price in advance, the person who is willing to roll up his sleeves and aggressively work for the prize he is seeking. Victory comes to the person who is willing to make a second effort after he falls short the first time around.

You've heard it so many times you probably don't want to hear it again. But it's still true, and it's still worth repeating: No pain, no gain. Behind every success, there is a lot of risk and a lot of planning. Behind every success, there is a lot of thought and a lot of due diligence. There may even be a lot of prayer. But one thing's for sure: Unless there's a lot of effort going into your dreams and your ventures, nothing will ever really happen. Success is an award for the aggressive.

In basketball and in life, "you have to learn the rules of the game, and then you have to play better than anyone else" (Albert Einstein). So learn from your past mistakes. Learn from your disappointments and failures, too. Find out what you did wrong or what went wrong, and work hard to keep those things from happening again. But once the deficiency has been corrected, put on your jersey and your shoes, stretch your muscles a little, get off the bench, and get back in the game. Playmakers are aggressive. They go hard after the ball, and they are willing to throw their bodies into the melee and to fight for the prize. So be the playmaker. Change the game. Change your life.

FEARLESSNESS

Courage is fear holding on a minute longer.
—George S. Patton

WHAT DO you fear? What holds you back? What is that one "thing" that creates a paralysis in your soul and causes you to avoid even thinking about the possibilities? Our fears are numerous, and our fears are diverse. Some of the most common fears we have are fears associated with the unknown, abandonment, ridicule, confinement, pain, disappointment, loneliness, rejection, failure, and death. We also are afraid of heights, snakes, spiders, water, flying, the dark, and speaking in public. So how do we ever get up enough courage to leave our houses?

I have found that, many times, imagined fears are more responsible for failure than any real actions a person may take. Just look at Tom as an example. Tom is friendly, talented, and intelligent, but Tom is afraid of the unknown. He is absolutely uncomfortable being in new situations outside his normal surroundings.

FACING YOUR FEARS HEAD-ON

When he was younger, Tom received a scholarship to attend a university four states away, and he attended that school for one semester. But Tom was so miserable at the university, he returned home and finished his degree at a local college. Now Tom is working, and he is good at his job. But he is not happy there. He has creative ideas and would actually like to start his own business. But he is afraid things might not work out for him. He wonders what he would do if sales should go down. And what if the economy should "tank" or he should hit a rough patch? What if …?

So Tom continues in his safe, unhappy position year after year, never achieving his full potential and never taking his big shot at life. His fears paralyze him and he fails to realize his deepest dreams, not because of what he does wrong, but simply because he does nothing.

As your coach, I'm telling you, face your fears and work through them. You may continue to be afraid, and you will certainly be aware of all the things that could go wrong. But do *not* let those thoughts and concerns keep you from taking your shot at life. In basketball terms, "get in the game."

Have you ever been to a huge arena where thousands of people have gathered to watch a professional sporting event like an NBA basketball game? If so, you've had a taste of what a professional athlete deals with every single day. You've heard the deafening cheers when the home team scores a big basket. You've heard the taunts and the jeers that the fans hurl at players on the opposing team. You've seen all the television cameras, and you've watched the replays on the big screens hanging over mid-court.

It would be a gross understatement to say that a professional basketball player is in the public eye. Actually, a professional basketball player is under a public microscope, especially during a game. Every move he makes is scrutinized, analyzed, and criticized to the point of exhaustion. And every mistake he makes is replayed on the late-night news and published for the world to see the following morning in newspapers across the nation. There may be a lot of fame that goes with playing the game of basketball, but the game brings far more criticism than praise. And it's the same way with life.

A lot of people are afraid to take a shot at their goals because they don't want to make a mistake. And they especially want to avoid making a mistake when the whole world is watching and everyone is just waiting for the opportunity to criticize them from the sidelines. But to be a winner, you have to learn to pursue your goals and to reject the fear that comes with the game.

From the sidelines, all we can see when we look at famous athletes and successful people is the splendor of success. From the stands, it all looks so glamorous—the cheers, the applause, the paparazzi, the limousines. But the view is quite different from center court during a game. The view is also different from the head chair in the boardroom and from the administrator's office at a major hospital or university. From the perspective of those who are running the race and competing for the prize, it feels like they're in a fishbowl with the whole world staring at their every move. And the fear can be stifling. It can be far more intimidating than others might imagine, especially if the person in the fishbowl has a past failure on his résumé or a missed shot that was the focus of the cover of *Sports Illustrated.* But that fear is exactly what you must overcome to be a winner.

PUSHING THROUGH YOUR FEARS

Let's look at what the Bible has to say about fear. Many men in the Bible were afraid. Think of Gideon in his battle against the Midianites. Think of David running for his life from King Saul. Think of Peter starting to sink below the waves of the storm-tossed sea. Many great men and women of faith faced tremendous inner fears, so there are numerous verses in the Bible that address the subject of fear. Here are just a few:

- Have I not commanded you? Be strong and courageous. Do not be afraid; do not be discouraged, for the LORD your God will be with you wherever you go. (Joshua 1:9, NIV)

- The LORD is my light and my salvation—whom shall I

fear? The LORD is the stronghold of my life—of whom shall I be afraid? (Psalm 27:1, NIV)

- When I am afraid, I put my trust in you. (Psalm 56:3, NIV)

- So we say with confidence, "The Lord is my helper; I will not be afraid. What can mere mortals do to me?" (Hebrews 13:6, NIV)

Therefore, consider these verses. The Lord of the universe tells you not to fear. He tells you that he will be with you when you face the fearful things of life. He is your light, and he is your helper. He is the one you can always trust when things ahead look frightening.

But how can you get past your fear? How can you break the stranglehold of anxiety and move forward with your life? Sometimes you are fearful because you don't know what is waiting for you, and other times you are fearful because you do. You've been there! You took the shot earlier and missed, and now you need to take another shot, but you know what happened the last time and you are doubly afraid of failing again. So what should you do? Let's take this one step at a time.

First, get out a piece of paper and get ready to write. At the top, give this little project a title: "When I think of being completely committed to my dream, I AM AFRAID OF …." Now, write down exactly what you are afraid might happen. What is it that is holding you back? When you think about stepping out, what causes you the most concern? What creates anxiety for you when you think about leaving your current comfort zone, whatever that might be?

You will only move forward when the thing you want to achieve becomes more important to you than the fear that is holding you back. So how badly do you want it? Let's look at four common fears you need to get past before you can make progress toward your goals.

Fear #1 — I've never done this before. It's outside my comfort zone, and the fear of the unknown is huge for me.
We touched on this approach to life with our references to Tom earlier in this chapter. Many people have some serious concerns about venturing into new places and being among people they do not know.

We are all creatures of habit. So if you pay close attention, you can probably recognize this tendency in your own life. When you go to the grocery store, for instance, or to the gym or to church, do you tend to park in the same spot every time? When you are invited to a social event, is it important to you to bring your spouse or a friend along with you? Would you go by yourself?

Fear of the unknown can hold you back from achieving a dream or a goal that is important to you. The world is large, and often, whether you like it or not, you will just have to expand your borders if you ever hope to do great things.

Think of the most important person in your life. Where did you meet that person? Most likely that person did not walk up to your front door and ring the doorbell. For the two of you to meet, at least one of you had to be in a place or a situation that was unfamiliar. But look at the benefits your life has gained by expanding your boundaries that day.

So what is more important to you, staying in your comfort zone or launching out on a lifetime adventure?

Fear #2 — I could fail.

Most people are afraid of failure and of the disappointment that goes along with it. But rebounding from a failure is even more frightening than the failure itself, because, while the pain from the first missed opportunity was bad enough, to miss again would be catastrophic. And if people criticized you following one failed attempt, how much more would those same people mock any additional efforts you might make?

On the basketball court and in life, the pain of failure is often crippling and the weight of unwarranted criticism is often destructive. And this is why so many people settle for mundane lives that bring them no fulfillment, especially if they have already failed once. Instead of facing the possible embarrassment of making a public mistake again, they decide to simply accept the runner-up trophy for a safe and predictable existence that takes them nowhere near their goals.

If you have ever watched a basketball game, you know that occasionally a player will take a shot and miss everything. There won't even be a rebound, because the ball won't make it to the rim. The shooter won't make contact with the backboard, the net, or any part of the goal, and the missed shot will fall embarrassingly short. In basketball, this is called an "air ball," because the ball hits nothing but air. And when a player from the visiting team shoots an "air ball," the fans in the stands start chanting, "Air ball! Air ball! Air ball!" For the next several minutes, every time that player touches the basketball, the spectators will start repeating in unison, "Air ball! Air ball! Air ball!"

The fans do this to remind the player of his recent failure and to intimidate the player in order to psychologically hinder him from taking another shot. But a good, confident player learns how to deal with this kind of pressure. He refuses to back down, and he refuses to let fear limit his actions. He believes in himself and his abilities, and he believes he can prevail if he just keeps taking the shot.

All of us have failed at something in our lives. All of us have made mistakes, and all of us have experienced the feelings that go along with efforts that yield no results. But if you have honestly tried to do something meaningful to push your dreams forward, then I commend you, because you have already distinguished yourself. You have already set yourself apart from the vast majority of people who will never even suit up and play the game.

Oh, they love to watch. They love to sit in the stands and scream their approval or disapproval. And when you succeed by hitting the big shot that wins the game, they will be among the first to ask for your autograph or to take a picture with you. They will brag about meeting you, and they will tell all their friends that the two of you are "tight." But they won't ever get in the game themselves, and they will criticize you every time you fall short of their demands.

So do you really need these fair-weather friends? Why not surround yourself instead with people who believe in you and who can help you get where you want to go? Why not surround yourself with people who understand the nature of the game: that it's not about perfection; it's about scoring. It's not about whether you hit the shot the first time or the tenth time; it's about whether you keep shooting until you score.

As I have explained, all of us have failed at something in our lives. If we have dared to shoot at something, we have missed once or twice. That's why Michael Jordan once said, "I have missed more than 9,000 shots in my career. I have lost almost 300 games. On 26 occasions, I have been entrusted to take the game winning shot ... and missed. And I have failed over and over and over again in my life. And that is why I succeed."

Jordan, like all other great players, knew how to rebound and to shoot again and again until he finally hit the target. He wouldn't give up. He wouldn't go away. He didn't even pay attention to the cheers and the jeers of the crowd. He just focused on the ball and focused on the rim and kept shooting and rebounding and shooting again until he finally overcame his misses and did what he was trying to do. He was fearless.

Charles Stanley says, "Fear stifles our thinking and actions. It creates indecisiveness that results in stagnation. I have known talented people who procrastinate indefinitely rather than risk failure. Lost opportunities cause erosion of confidence, and the downward spiral begins." So don't let the fear of failure hold you back from the best of your life.

Fear #3 — People might criticize, ridicule, and reject me.

Think about this twisted logic for a minute. Do you really believe that the people you love and trust are going to laugh at you or belittle you if you should fail to achieve something that is important to you? Would you laugh at them or ridicule them if they failed to achieve their goals? Is this kind of fear actually based on reality, or is it just a monster hiding in the closet of your imagination?

People fear a lot of things when they think about pursuing the best that life has to offer them, just as basketball players fear a lot of things when they think about the next big game. But fear is more about a person's imagination than the facts. And chief among people's fears is the fear of criticism. People are simply afraid of looking foolish in front of other people, especially when those other people have already predicted their downfall. People are afraid of rejection.

And it's understandable that people would fear this kind of rejection by others, even though it's illogical. After all, when you think back over your life, you can probably recall a lot of times when the people on the fringes of your life tried to discourage you from pursuing your dreams, or they made fun of you when you failed to do the ambitious things you said you were going to do. You can probably recall several occasions when the people on the outer rings of your life doubted your ability to excel or openly mocked others who had failed, leading you to believe they would mock you, too, if you should take a shot and miss.

But the reality of life is that most of the people who know you have supported you with their words. Most of the people who love you have believed in you through thick and thin. It's the people on the periphery of your life—the spectators—who are disinclined to believe in you. Like the fans watching a basketball game from the upper-level seats, they will cheer for you when you're on top of your game, but they will mock you and ridicule you whenever you miss a big shot. And they will constantly offer their advice from the safety and security of their padded chairs.

For some reason, however, it matters to a lot of us what these people think. For some reason, a lot of us are anxiously seeking the approval of these "spectators." Unfortunately, if you are waiting for the spectators in the stands to start believing in you before you even believe in yourself, you might as well take off your uniform and make plans to retire from the sport. You might as well call it quits, because the spectators in life will never understand or appreciate those of us who are truly engaged in the game.

So try to keep things in perspective. Those people who may criticize you from the sidelines are people who don't really matter anyway. They are people who will casually cross your path for a moment in time, and then vanish over the horizon into the misty memories of the past. They are people whose attitudes and expectations are distorted by their own personal failures. They have fallen short of their own goals in life, so they have decided to quit instead of taking another shot at their dreams. And that's why these peripheral people don't have anything better to do with their time than to voice their disapproval of you and others who still have a chance to succeed and who are still trying to get in the game and make a difference.

Scoffers are people who used to dream, but now they live in the safety, security, and predictability of their own mediocre little worlds because they failed once and they are afraid to try again. And subconsciously, they don't want you to try again either, because your success would be an indictment of their own submission to fear. Scoffers are people who want you to conform to their mediocrity.

But don't. Ignore the criticism and the pessimism of those people on the fringes of your life. Draw your encouragement and your support instead from those who know you best and who believe in you. And do something meaningful with your life so you won't become a pessimist yourself, judging the performance of others from the safety of the bleachers while you secretly regret never playing the game.

And don't be concerned about how you look to others, either. Instead, become more concerned about your goals than you are about what others think. Lou Brock, the great baseball Hall of Famer, once said, "Show me a guy who's afraid to look bad, and I'll show you a guy you can beat every time."

The people who have done notable things with their lives aren't the ones who are mocking you or discouraging you. It's the do-nothings and the wannabes who are criticizing you for taking action while they sink deeper into their sofas to watch others perform great feats on television. So don't be afraid of their criticism. And remember what's driving their words.

Fear #4 — I might get hurt, maybe emotionally, perhaps financially.
Yes, you might. But you might not. Do the benefits outweigh the risks? Would you prefer to sit immobile, watching others play the game, wishing it were you and wondering what might have been? Or would you rather take a shot at greatness even though you run the risk of incurring a few bumps and bruises?

Regardless of what you decide, I'll tell you this: If you have set some goals for yourself and some dreams that are worthy of your pursuit, you will definitely not reach those goals unscathed. You will definitely not realize those dreams without feeling some pain. Somewhere along the way, you *will* be hurt. You will be knocked off your feet, and you will feel real agony. But that does not give you a reason to quit. Instead, it gives you a reason to move on and to push through the trial.

Consider the rebounder. What if a basketball player should say to his coach, "You know, Coach, last time I got the ball, I shot and missed. That was a failure. And I heard the crowd booing me. I also took an elbow to the ribs, and that really hurt. So, I'm done. Count me out. I'll just sit on the bench over here and watch everyone else play the game"?

It sounds quite silly to think that a tall, talented, athletic young man would have this kind of attitude about trying again. But does it sound any less silly to hear a talented person, created with vast potential in the image and likeness of God, set aside his ideals and dreams, saying, "I can't do it. I'm afraid. What if ... ?"

C. Joybell, the Scottish journalist and author, said, "Don't be afraid of your fears. They're not there to scare you. They're there to let you know that something is worth it."

And something is indeed worth it. If it's in your heart and it won't go away and you can't find satisfaction until you do something about it, then that dream within your heart is God's destiny for your life. Don't expect its achievement to be easy. Expect the battle for that worthy prize to be difficult and lengthy. Expect opposition to stand between you and its attainment. Expect criticism from the fans in the stands. And expect the cameras to record your every ill-timed move and your every misstep along the way.

But don't let these things deter you. Don't let them discourage you or daunt you. Go for it. Take the shot. Do something about that business opportunity that's in front of you. Pursue that college degree if it will help you get where you want to go. Write that book you've always wanted to write. Record that song. Launch that ministry. Quit talking about it, quit worrying about it, quit thinking about it, and just do it.

The world rewards action, not thought. Even though we admire people who can dream and even though we highly esteem the great thinkers, philosophers, and pundits who put forth noble ideas, the world has always been most impressed by those who can actually move beyond the thinking stage and do something notable with their lives, because people of action are fearless people. So on the basketball court and in life, we admire those who can bounce back because they aren't afraid of the opposition. We admire those who can rebound because they aren't deterred by the criticism or the risk of failing again. We admire those who just keep working and who just keep trying. And we admire them because eventually they always manage to win.

EFFORT

THE BASICS OF THE GAME

PREPARATION

Lack of confidence is born from a lack of preparation.
—Shannon Wilburn

OR AN ATHLETE, preparation consists of two different, yet complementary actions. A world-class athlete must prepare his mind, and he must prepare his body as well.

An athlete can have incredible natural abilities, and most professional athletes do. But without the kind of preparation that gives that athlete knowledge of the game and knowledge of the opposition, his natural abilities will only carry him so far. On the other hand, that same athlete can know his sport "inside and out," and he can be completely informed about his opponent, but without the physical preparation to back his mental preparedness, he is still destined to lose.

Both mental and physical preparation are critical for success. You must learn, therefore, and you must practice. You must gain knowledge, and you must gain the practical experience that can give substance to the knowledge you have attained.

WHY PREPARATION IS SO IMPORTANT

As a success coach, I see the need every day for prior planning. People fail because they did not prepare. They fail because they move forward before they have the knowledge necessary to do so. The old saying, "Look before you leap," is quite true, but so is another old saying, "Learn before you leap."

In fact, learn everything you can about your specific area of passion before you commit yourself to that passion. Learn about your competition, too. Learn about the economic factors affecting your dream, learn about the people involved, do your homework, and analyze the facts before you take that plunge. Armies do not march off to war without an enormous amount of pre-planning and preparation. Olympians do not participate in their individual sports without investing an astonishing quantity of time in training and conditioning. So set a reasonable timeframe to prepare for action; then take action and press relentlessly toward your goal.

In Luke 14:28, Jesus said, "Is there anyone here who, planning to build a new house, doesn't first sit down and figure the cost so you'll know if you can complete it? If you only get the foundation laid and then run out of money, you're going to look pretty foolish. Everyone passing by will poke fun at you: 'He started something he couldn't finish'" (MSG). Too often, however, the lure of the goal causes us to get ahead of ourselves and to jump off the diving board before we are ready. Too often, our hearts get ahead of our heads.

If you know me, you know that I'm not one to procrastinate, because the world rewards action, not endless thought and planning. But I would caution you against moving too quickly. Impulsive behavior is often worse than no behavior at all. Yes, you want to get started. Yes, you need to see some results. And yes, you need to do something to actually get the process moving, because God always blesses "something"; he never blesses "nothing."

But preparation is what will set you apart and make your actions fruitful. Being organized, informed, and equipped for success is what will make you successful and what will pay off many times over. Your foundation of knowledge and practice will give you a distinct advantage over your competition and will propel you to the forefront of success. So get ready to prepare. It's what winners do.

Preparation gives you confidence. Recently, the daughter of a friend of mine graduated from college, and she was about to interview for her first real job. Her father said, "Janna, you need to do some preparation. You can't just go in there cold. I have hired people at my company for years and have been through the interview process several times myself. Let me help you identify the questions you may be asked, and let's work together on a strategy of how you should present yourself in this interview."

So for several days, father and daughter sat together to review possible questions, to research the company where Janna would be interviewing, to discuss the best answers to showcase her skills, and even to engage in some mock interviews where my friend played the role of the potential employer. And when Janna's interview day finally arrived, she was well equipped and had the confidence of being on familiar ground because of the time spent preparing. Consequently, her interview went extremely well and she was offered the job, returning home to tell my friend, "Dad, it was just like you said. Several of the questions were the exact ones we used in practice, so I knew precisely what to say."

This is a simple example and I wouldn't want to suggest that all of life's challenges are this easy, but the principles are there to see. Preparedness breeds confidence, and confidence breeds results. For a team to win enough games to get into the playoffs and enough playoff games to become world champions, a coach and his players must approach every game with a sense of urgency. This means the coach must prepare his team by carefully studying the plays and the probable strategies of the opposing team. And each player must prepare by diligently analyzing the moves and the expected tactics of the individual opponent he will be facing.

But without preparation, there can be no championship. A team that can execute well is destined to win a few ballgames simply by virtue of their skill, and a player who has all the right moves is destined to hit a few game-winning shots simply by virtue of his talent. In fact, a talented player will hit a lot of big shots, and a team with skilled players will prevail in a whole lot of ballgames. But neither a player nor a team can consistently win on the basketball court, regardless of talent and experience, without preparing for the opponents they must face. Winning is not achieved by relying on talent alone. Likewise, a person cannot prevail in life by relying solely on his abilities or his past achievements. Preparation is essential.

Bobby Knight, the former head basketball coach who won three national championships at the University of Indiana, said, "The key is not the will to win. Everybody has that. It is the will to *prepare* to win that is important." So to be a great player, you must gain the knowledge you need to win on the court. You must understand what you can and can't do, and you must understand what your opponent can and can't do. And then you must develop a workable plan and go out on the court to execute that plan in a way that takes advantage of the knowledge you have gained.

PREPARING THE MIND BY LEARNING

Knowledge is the foundation of success in sports. It is the precursor to talent. It is the underlying commodity that makes success possible for those who have talent and those who can showcase their talents on the field of play. It is the common thread that runs through the career of every Hall of Famer and the history of every great team.

Just think about it! Before a coach takes his team on the court, he spends countless hours wading through scouting reports and watching video of the opposing team in action. He reviews statistics, and he and his staff pore over the observations of sportscasters and other coaches who have faced the team that he and his squad will be facing on Saturday. Then, based on the information he has gained, the coach develops a plan of attack that will enable him to utilize his team's greatest strengths while taking advantage of his opponent's biggest weaknesses.

The coach spent the preseason working on execution with his players. He spent the weeks prior to the season's first game helping his players master the fundamentals. He spent the initial practice sessions instilling in his players the kind of attitude that would enable them to prevail in competition. But before sending those talented players onto the court to execute what they have learned, he develops a strategy. He develops a carefully laid plan for each approaching game. And he builds that plan around the knowledge he gains while preparing for the game.

So knowledge is power. People who are successful know things that other people just don't know. They know more about their professional subject matter than the other people in that profession. They know more about the laws that affect them than others who are impacted by those laws. They know more about politics in the workplace than the other workers in their company. They know more about the key players in their fields of labor. They know more about the latest trends in the market and in technology. And they know more about solutions that work, because knowledge is power. In fact, knowledge is more powerful than money or a fancy title or the connections a person might have in the marketplace of competition. Knowledge opens the pathway to everything that matters.

Consider this! Why do you pay a mechanic hundreds of dollars to fix an oil leak in your car? Because he knows how to fix it, and you don't! Why do you pay a doctor hundreds of dollars just to check your vital signs and write you a prescription? Because he knows what is causing your fever and what drug can best cure it, and you don't! Why do you spend hundreds of dollars to attend a rock concert? Because your favorite band knows how to write music and perform it in a way that moves you, and you don't!

People who know things succeed; people who don't know things fail. So a wise man will continue to learn throughout his life. He will seek knowledge and wisdom from every worthy source. He will constantly add new facts to the information he already possesses. He will attend seminars, listen to lectures, go to school at night, and read books. Perhaps that is why poor people have big televisions while wealthy people have big libraries. The man who wants to succeed, particularly in the wake of past failures, is the man who will do whatever it takes to gather the information he needs in order to grow, to change, and to flourish in the areas of life that interest him.

If you have failed in the past at any endeavor that was important to you—marriage, business, investment, or anything else— you probably failed not because you lacked the ability to execute your plan and not because you lacked the talent to succeed, but because you lacked the knowledge you needed to develop the right kind of plan to seize the opportunity. You failed because you did not have the information you needed to succeed. You failed because you lacked an adequate understanding of the challenges that confronted you and the best way to meet those challenges head-on.

In life, as in basketball, defeat can often be linked to a lack of knowledge. It can often be connected to a lack of preparation. People fail not from a lack of talent or ambition and not from a lack of vision, but rather because they do not understand what they are up against or they fail to grasp the difficulty of the challenge that awaits them.

It is a statistical fact in this country that only one person in a hundred will become wealthy as a result of his labor. It is a statistical fact that only three people in a hundred will become financially secure, though not necessarily wealthy. This means that 96 percent of the people who set out with a confident attitude about the future and a buoyant swagger to their step will end up falling short of their financial goals. They will fail to achieve what they expected to achieve when they were younger and inexperienced.

But this high rate of failure cannot be attributed to a lack of talent, because all these people showed talent when they started their journey. And this high rate of failure cannot be attributed to a lack of motivation, because Americans work harder and work longer hours than any other people in the world. This high rate of failure can only be attributed to a lack of knowledge. People in this country often take up a pursuit without adequately understanding the challenges that await them or the costs they must pay. They undertake a mission without an accurate appraisal of the competition they will confront or the risks they will encounter. Thus, many people fall short of reaching their goals.

So, if you have failed in the past and you want to succeed in the future, you must understand the obstacles that await you. And as you recover from the missed shots of the past, you must be careful not to march blindly into battle with the same gullible or half-informed approach that caused you to fall short of your goals the first time around. Instead, do what good rebounders do, and prepare yourself for the challenge ahead. Understand the nature of the conflict, and understand the costs you must pay in order to prevail. Know your competition, and have a plan that addresses every possible contingency.

John Wooden was probably the greatest college basketball coach of all time. He won an unprecedented ten national championships at UCLA (seven in a row). And he coached some of the greatest players in the game, rebounders like Kareem Abdul-Jabbar and Bill Walton and three-point shooters like Reggie Miller. But Coach Wooden was more than just a basketball coach. He was a mentor. He prepared his players for victory in life as much as he prepared them for victory on the court. And Wooden believed in learning. He believed in the power of knowledge. Wooden often told his players, "If I'm through learning, I'm through."

PREPARING THE BODY BY PRACTICING

Like the game of basketball, life is made up of thousands of little decisions and thousands of little moves that come together to create a picture of one's achievements and future capabilities. So this is where the preparation of both the mind and the body comes into play.

The primary task of the coach is to educate and train while the primary task of the athlete is to learn and rehearse. In the game of life, as in the game of basketball, greatness is the progeny of the union of knowledge and practice. It is the offspring of learning and rehearsing. As a coach teaches and as an athlete practices, the skills that are necessary for success become imbedded in the player's body and mind, making him a fine-tuned "machine" of perfected execution. And victory is the result.

As Coach Bobby Knight has often explained, practice structure determines success. To succeed, you must put your knowledge to work. And to put your knowledge to work, you must practice, because practice provides experience. Anyone who has tried to become great—in a sport, in playing an instrument, or in some other pursuit—can certainly relate to Bobby Knight's formula. He also can relate to Joyce Meyer's statement, "The way anything is developed is through practice, practice, practice, practice, practice, practice, practice, practice, practice, and more practice."

So obviously, although knowledge can be gained from a formal education and although you may need some more formal education before taking your next shot, the most useful knowledge you will accumulate in your lifetime is the knowledge you gain off-campus after graduation. There is simply no substitute for experience. A soldier can graduate boot camp with honors. But when he faces hostile fire on the battlefield for the very first time, that soldier will quickly learn things he could never possibly learn in a military classroom or some other controlled environment, and he will rapidly become what they call "battle-hardened."

The same is true for you: You definitely need academic information regarding the things you plan to do. But you also need some practical experience, and you need the input of those who have made the journey ahead of you. You need one or more mentors, and you need a network of knowledgeable and experienced people around you who can encourage you when you are down, hold you in check when you are too eager, and share firsthand knowledge with you that could never be gleaned from any other source.

Professional basketball is like many other endeavors that make up this thing called "life." A lot goes on behind the scenes that the average person does not see. Obviously, you and I see the razzle-dazzle associated with the game. We see the cheerleaders and the large crowds. We read the newspaper articles about the huge salaries and the excessive lifestyles of the athletes who play the game. We see the television commercials that carry the endorsements of the players, and we read about the personality clashes in the locker room and the personal tragedies that mark the lives of the public figures in the sport.

But what we don't get to see is what goes on behind the scenes. Behind the scenes, there are really two kinds of players. There is the player who relies on his talent and his reputation, the player who thinks he is great and who rides the wave of fame and fortune for as long as he can get away with it. But in the end, this player doesn't go very far. He doesn't achieve very much. He doesn't meet the high expectations of his team or the fans, and he slowly fades away. Then there is the player who learns everything he can possibly learn about the game, his opponents, and his own teammates' abilities. This player couples his newfound knowledge with the hard work that is associated with endless hours of practice, and he comes to the games fully prepared. This is the player who lasts.

And the parallel here between the world of athletic competition and real life is amazing, because there are two kinds of "life players," as well. There is the life player who attempts to succeed through connections, through charm and charisma, through bluffing, or through doing just enough to get by. But in time, without substance, this person always fades away. Then there is the person who avidly seeks knowledge, who learns everything he can learn and applies that knowledge to his life. He works long hours, and he works diligently, many times in the face of opposition and criticism. But he has the will to prepare, the work ethic to support his dreams and goals, and a clear vision of what he wants to achieve. He is the man who will endure.

History's greatest basketball players earned their spots in the Hall of Fame not by doing everything perfectly, but by prevailing in their struggles against the obstacles, the setbacks, the challenges, and the opposition that stood between them and their goals. Literally! So a player's career does not rise or fall on one shot, even though each shot is important. But a player's career consists of multiple seasons, and a season consists of multiple games, and a game consists of a whole lot of individual battles involving a whole lot of shots, rebounds, passes, and defensive moves.

Greatness, therefore, is built piece by piece, and the key to a successful career is for a player to do all the little things with excellence on a cumulative basis. The key to a successful career is for a player to execute every move to the best of his ability during every play of every game. Then, once the game is won, he can move on to the next game and the next, until the season is finally won. And once the season is won, he can move on to the following season and so on, until his name and his accomplishments are seared in the public consciousness.

Similarly, the key to success in life is to do all the little things well and to do them every single day. Great things are made up of a whole lot of little things. So to have a great life, all your weeks, days, and irretrievable moments must be lived with purpose and excellence. Your minutes and hours must become the building blocks of your greater destiny. So make them worthy.

To be a champion, an ambitious athlete must learn how to do all the little things with excellence and consistency, and he must hone his craft by learning from others. He must mimic the habits of the legends who have already done what he wants to do in the sport. He must listen to those with experience who can aid him in his development as a player. And the same is true in life. Rebounding in life is about understanding your situation. It's about experience and the careful guidance of knowledgeable people who can help you snap back from a loss.

This means that as you contemplate the reasons behind your missed shots of the past, you must realize that you need to do something different with your next shot. You need to position yourself better. And to do so, you must have a better understanding of your challenges and the obstacles that confront you. You must know your competition better. You must better understand your own abilities and limitations. And you must have a game plan. You cannot win at basketball or life by simply playing the game and hoping for the outcome you want.

So if you have missed more shots than you have made in life or if you have missed the big, important shots that caused you to lose in the final seconds of a championship game, find out what it is you do not know. Determine what you need to know to improve your game and to score in a big way your next time out. Read, study, prepare, and do your research and your due diligence. And perhaps most importantly, surround yourself with people who have already done what you want to do or people who have done it better.

Learn from others and learn from life. Then put that knowledge to work and gain the practical experience in your field of competition that you need to survive and to thrive. And practice, practice, practice! When you do, you will move forward with the confidence that only comes from being fully prepared for success.

———————————————————

POSITIONING

First, master the fundamentals.

—Larry Bird

WHERE YOU place yourself determines your level of success. To succeed in any endeavor, you must position yourself in a way that maximizes your potential for success in that effort. To fail, you need only to position yourself in a way that makes success less likely.

Recently, I took my son, Solomon, to a baseball game where he desperately wanted to catch a fly ball. So we sat in the stands along the third base line, in a very opportune location for catching foul balls. And indeed, Solomon did realize his dream. He caught not one, but two baseballs that afternoon. But those memorable moments were created because we intentionally placed ourselves in a position to maximize success. If we had sat behind the backstop or out in right field, our day would most likely have ended without achieving the goal Solomon wanted to achieve. The same is true in other areas of life. Where you place yourself goes a long way in determining whether you succeed or fail.

In the opening chapter of this book, I mentioned Dennis Rodman, a former pro basketball player who currently ranks twenty-second on the list of all-time rebounders. Rodman was noted for his determination, and he was consumed with rebounding the basketball. According to his own assessment of his contributions to his team, Rodman would jump three or four times for a loose ball while some of the other players would only jump once.

But what really made Rodman great was that he learned to fill a role that served the best interests of his team. Obviously, Rodman was a superb athlete with tremendous physical abilities. On any other team, he might have been the leading rebounder of all time. But Rodman wasn't interested in racking up individual numbers for the record books; he was interested in winning. And that is why Rodman's twenty-second-place ranking as an individual rebounder doesn't come close to adequately describing his value as a player. Rodman was the centerpiece of a team that was one of the greatest in NBA history.

Dennis Rodman played for the Chicago Bulls. But not just any Chicago Bulls team! He played for the team that won three back-to-back NBA championships, the team that was packed with world-class players like Michael Jordan and Scottie Pippen. But while Rodman quietly went about his business, winning seven straight NBA rebounding titles (three of them with Chicago), Pippen and Jordan got most of the attention because they scored most of the points.

Nevertheless, Rodman was the player who made many of those points possible. And during his first season with the Bulls, he helped his team win 72 of their regular-season games, a record that still stands to this day. Rodman was the player that would climb the wall if necessary to retrieve a missed shot and then pass it back out so that the team's star players could take a second shot at the goal.

Quite often, Rodman was asked about the role that he played on that almost unbeatable team. As would be expected, he gave most of the credit to his team's reliable scorers, and he gave credit to his coach and to the other athletes who helped set up the plays that typically led to a Ron Harper jump shot or a Michael Jordan slam dunk. But regarding his position on the squad, Rodman explained that he had to play a different role in Chicago than he had played elsewhere in the NBA. While his teammates needed to be optimistic, expecting all their plays to work, Rodman had to be the sole pessimist on the floor, expecting none of the plays to work. While the fans in the stands would rise to their feet in expectation of a great shot by Jordan, Pippen, Harper, or Longley, Rodman would plant his feet in the expectation that those guys were going to miss their shots and he would have to come down with the rebound.

In fact, Rodman once said that he expected Michael Jordan to miss every shot that he took. And that is the reason why Rodman was such a great rebounder and why the Chicago Bulls were so hard to defeat. Rodman's anticipation that his fellow players were going to miss their shots motivated him to position himself for the rebound on every shot. Obviously, Rodman hoped for the best, but he was prepared for the worst. As the man responsible for retrieving missed shots, he was always mentally prepared and physically positioned to take possession of the basketball if the shot should fall short or drift long. Strong positioning is the essential factor in successful rebounding.

So, how can you create a strong position? How can you know where to be and what to do in order to maximize your potential for success? I believe there are three necessary disciplines associated with positioning that every successful person must grasp. And as your success coach, I want to share these three disciplines with you. I also want to share with you a few probing questions that you should consider as you absorb these concepts. Use these questions as an assessment tool to help you determine your own position in life and to discover ways that you can better position yourself to achieve your goals.

First, to be positioned for greatness, you must be ready. To succeed at anything worthwhile, you must prepare yourself through education. As we discussed in the previous chapter, knowledge is a key factor in winning, and knowledge is essential for proper positioning. A person cannot properly position himself for success in competition or in life until that person knows the things that he needs to know. Rodman, for instance, knew that 75 percent of all missed shots bounce *away* from the shooter. He knew that the longer the shot, the higher and harder the ball tends to bounce off the backboard or the rim.

Of course, not everything in basketball can be accurately predicted in advance. Not everything in life can be accurately predicted either. If all things could be perfectly forecast in the game of basketball, then talent, drive, and preparation would not be required to win games. And the same is true in life. But a serious player who has studied the game of basketball knows that certain things are more likely to occur than other things. Certain players are more likely to take a shot. Certain shots are more likely to go through the hoop. Certain types of shots come off the rim harder. Certain body language indicates the likelihood of a particular offensive play. And certain players will usually fake a shot before passing the ball inside.

To be positioned for success, therefore, a player needs to know that the opposing coach usually follows a timeout with a particular defensive strategy. He needs to know that his own coach is planning to put shorter players in the lineup during the next break in the action so his team can apply full-court pressure during the waning moments of the game. He even needs to know that the opposing team's management tends to keep the temperature slightly hot in their home arena in order to tire the visiting team more quickly. All this knowledge contributes to a player's ability to position himself properly so he can rebound or shoot the basketball. There is simply no way to overemphasize the value of information, because correct information leads to correct positioning.

When I was young, I failed at business. I made a million dollars, and then I lost a million dollars. In fact, I lost more money in the long run than I made. Like so many people, I started out red-hot. I was making more money than I had ever dreamed of making. But eventually, my lack of knowledge and my poor positioning overcame my raw talent and enthusiasm, and the realities of competition caught up with me. I got my butt kicked, and I failed miserably because all the things I didn't know when I first started out eventually came back to haunt me.

But I didn't let that setback destroy me. I embraced it as a learning experience, and I began to seek the knowledge I would need before trying my hand at business once more. So I started studying anything and everything I could put my hands on. I read books. I listened to CDs. I also surrounded myself with people who knew the kinds of things I wanted to know. And today, not only do I have a lot of successful friends who advise me and motivate me; I also have a large library in my house that is chock-full of information related to my various fields of interest.

But I certainly don't consider the small fortune I spent on that library to be a waste of my resources. Rather, I consider it to be an investment, because one of my goals in life is to learn something new every day. If I build my knowledge base daily, I am positioning myself for success. What about you? Are you learning? Are you asking questions?

One relevant and critical question to ask yourself is, "Am I teachable?" Too many athletes never realize their full potential in their sport because they are unwilling to be coached. They arrive at the court or the field with supreme confidence in their own abilities and the misplaced belief that they have all the knowledge necessary for winning. Their inability to receive constructive criticism and their refusal to submit to the authority of the coach creates a person whose value is so diminished that his athletic contribution is nullified.

Years ago, a friend told me the story of his final high school football game, where the coach had called a certain play. As a seventeen-year-old high school senior, my friend thought he could do better than the coach, so in the huddle he changed the play. Fortunately, the team pulled off the altered play, and they scored. And as he was relating the story to me, I realized that my friend was still rather pleased with himself for the choice he had made.

But I had a completely different take on the whole situation, because, as a coach, I know how lethal a person can be who cannot follow instructions. The results of self-focus and pride are destructive, and that play could have just as easily turned sour. If the play called by the coach had failed, the frustration of the fans would have been directed at the coach, not the players. As it was, however, this youthful and rebellious quarterback pulled off a successful switcheroo. And it was good for him that this happened during his last game of his last year, because he would never have started as quarterback the following year. That player lost his value to the team and to his coach, because he was no longer teachable.

You do not know everything. You have not lived through every experience, and you have not accumulated every tidbit of wisdom and knowledge. So be a learner. Be a listener. Be willing to glean information from the experiences of others. Be teachable.

Other factors to consider as you ready yourself for greatness are your current obligations and your finances. Are you overburdened? Are you in debt? Too many people miss out on opportunities to pursue their greatest passions because they are burdened down with debt. For these people, the accumulation of "bigger and better" has created a prison of monetary obligations that has become so overwhelming the notion of freedom is a completely pointless idea.

Excessive debt can be a dream killer. So if you find your dreams being put on hold and your passions taking a back seat to boredom because you cannot financially afford to make the changes you need to make in your life, you need to stop and reevaluate your priorities and your spending habits. Determine once and for all what is important to you. Then develop and strictly maintain a plan to pay off your debt so you can make the necessary changes that will make your dreams attainable. To be positioned for greatness, you must be in control of your own destiny. But the heavy shackles of financial bondage can make it absolutely impossible to even position yourself for a shot at greatness.

Second, to be positioned for greatness, you must be willing to work. As we have seen, the pursuit of education and knowledge takes a serious and concerted effort, and proper positioning requires hard work. In fact, work is a life principle that we seem to continually revisit in this text. So let me be very clear: Without hard work, you will never accomplish any worthwhile dream or achieve any worthwhile goal. That's right! Whether in life or in sports, without a strong work ethic, you can look forward to getting left in the dust.

A lot of people achieve success through hard work and sacrifice, but many others reap the benefits of other people's toil. Perhaps their fathers, spouses, or business partners were the ones who put in the long hours to produce the prosperous lifestyles that these people enjoy. If you are the beneficiary of someone else's efforts, consider yourself blessed and let the knowledge of that fact motivate you to continue the practice of blessing other people through your own diligent efforts.

But regardless of whether you are trying to build your own life or enrich the lives of others, never succumb to the temptation to "settle." Never be a simple consumer who just sucks up all the air without adding something to the people who are part of your life and to your community, your country, and the world. And do not be one who devours what your predecessors have provided for you without making the benefits of your own industriousness available to those who come after you. Work is God-given. In the Garden of Eden, the only perfect place the world has ever known, God gave Adam work to do.

That's right! According to Genesis 2:15, "the LORD God took the man and put him in the Garden of Eden *to work it* and take care of it" (NIV, emphasis mine). So work is not part of the curse, because God made man and gave him the gift of work long before God pronounced his curse on the earth and mankind. Besides, the curse that eventually came as God's response to man's disobedience was not a curse that was directed at the institution of work itself. The curse was a pronouncement regarding the obstacles and hindrances that would be added to man's life in order to make his work more difficult and his efforts less productive. Work itself has always been godly and noble.

So success comes from hard work. Are you willing to do a lot of hard work? Success comes from effort. Are you committed to investing sweat equity in your dreams?

Ray Kroc, the man who built McDonald's into the most successful fast-food operation in the world, said, "The two most important requirements for major success are first, being in the right place at the right time, and second, doing something about it." If you want to win, you must "do something about it." Simply put, you must work.

Dennis Rodman pulled down a lot of key rebounds to feed back outside to Michael Jordan at critical moments in critical games, and those rebounds allowed the Chicago Bulls to dominate professional basketball during the late 1990s. So Dennis Rodman was renowned for being in the right place at the right time. But the "secret" to Rodman's instinct for proper positioning was his willingness to put in the work that was necessary for establishing proper position in the first place. So Rodman did what was necessary to obtain the knowledge he needed to position himself properly, and he became the sport's key player "in the paint." Thus, while the fans rushed to get Michael Jordan's autograph after the game and while the sportscasters lined up to interview the top scorers and playmakers, Rodman knew in his heart that he was the "secret" behind the team's success and he was the guy who made a lot of those amazing victories possible. He made the rest of his teammates and his coach look really, really good.

Often, the things that turn us into champions are the things that other people don't notice. They are the things that are done behind closed doors. Often, the things that bring us success are the things that other people don't applaud, because other people can't see them and can't appreciate their worth. But as Coach Roy Barsh from Southeastern University often tells me, "While the results of success are praised in public, the process of success is endured alone."

So there is no success without the process, and the process is called "work." There is no reward in the "get-rich-quick" schemes that are part of everyday life, because true reward is found instead in the things that occupy our hands and our minds through labor. As Colin Powell says, "A dream doesn't become reality through magic; it takes sweat, determination, and hard work."

Third, to be positioned for greatness, you must be willing to change. Proper positioning requires continual assessment and movement. Your position can never be static; you must maintain alertness. The willingness to change, therefore, will be a key factor in your ability to reach your goals. Time changes, technology changes, circumstances change, and you, too, must be willing to adapt to the shifting climate that surrounds you if you intend to stay relevant and competitive.

In 2012, just prior to Kodak filing for bankruptcy protection, *Forbes* magazine published an article entitled, "How Kodak Failed." In the article, *Forbes* detailed a sobering look at the decisions made by Kodak management that kept them outside the ever-exploding digital market when that market began to take over the photography industry. But the glaring irony in Kodak's decision to avoid the emerging digital market is the fact that a Kodak engineer actually invented the digital camera in 1975.

According to the article, Steve Sasson, the engineer who created the digital camera, described the company's initial response to his invention as rather indifferent. According to Sasson, the leaders of Kodak were disappointed that the new camera did not utilize film photography, and their attitude was "that's cute—but don't tell anyone about it."

Then, in 1981, Vince Barabba, the head of Kodak's market intelligence, conducted some extensive research designed to predict the future of film photography in relation to its digital competition. And following his research, Barabba informed Kodak that they had a 10-year window to prepare for the market swing away from film and toward digital photography. But Kodak executives ignored Barabba's findings, further undermining their future status as a viable company by deciding not to alter their company's commitment to film. A decade later, however, digital photography stormed the market, causing Kodak to fall steadily behind its competition. And when other poor management decisions contributed to its further decline, Kodak, an American icon for 124 years, finally filed for Chapter 11 bankruptcy protection.

Are you willing to adapt? Are you in the right location for your dream to prosper? Do you have the right employees? Do you have the most effective mentors?

I want to be very clear on this topic of change. Being willing and open to position yourself for success means that your methods must sometimes change, even though your message will remain the same. While your way of conducting business must adapt to changing conditions, your core principles—the heart principles—should never change to match the conditions around you. Principles of honesty, integrity, loyalty, and courage must remain consistent throughout your life and your career, because methods change, but meaningful goals and the internal mechanisms that give rise to those goals can never be altered for the sake of convenience.

In basketball, the fundamentals never change either, but other things never stop changing. So placing yourself in an optimal position for the rebound requires constant assessment and ceaseless movement that is always dependent on the location of that bouncing ball. To win at basketball, therefore, a good player and a good coach must know the difference between those things that are fundamental and those things that are "fluid," and the team and the coach must adjust themselves accordingly.

To be positioned for greatness, you too must be ready to respond to the changing circumstances around you and you must be willing to prepare yourself for the inevitable changes that will come. You also must be willing to work so you can take advantage of the opportunities that change will place before you. And when you come to the point where you can consistently do these things in your life and your career, you will definitely stand out from the crowd. You will definitely be recognized and celebrated for what you do, and what you do will be so outstanding that it elevates you above all those around you. In other words, you will be noticed because you will be different, and you will different because you will be positioned to succeed.

You are unique. There's no one like you in all the world. You need to know that, and you need to show that. You may need to change some of the ways that you do things so you can stay relative and on the cutting edge. But you never need to change who you are. You never need to change your core principles, your core dreams, or your unique approach to life that makes you different from everybody else around you. Instead, you need to embrace your "difference" and use it. And you need to embrace the unchanging qualities of greatness that will set you apart from the masses.

As an employee, would you like to be noticed? Then always be on time, always be prepared, and always work harder than anyone else in the company. If you do, you will certainly be identified as a remarkable employee, and you will position yourself for favor.

As a manger, do you stand out? Do you lead by building up your employees instead of tearing them down? Do you share the workload with them? Are you known for dispensing praise and shouldering responsibility instead of passing the buck and making excuses?

As a friend or family member, are you different? Do you keep confidences? Do you encourage those who need your support? Do you compliment rather than criticize? What makes you great? What sets you apart from the crowd?

Standing out from all the rest is a result of intentional, dedicated positioning, and it is vital in the journey toward greatness. The victorious athletes and the successful individuals who make a difference in their sports and in the world are those who distinguish themselves through knowledge, hard work, and adaptability. They are the ones who set themselves apart through preparation in every area of their lives. They are the ones who remember that positioning determines success and that a person's decisions regarding how he will position himself for the future have everything to do with the kind of future that he writes for his own life.

So be like those who repeatedly win in basketball and in life. Position yourself for victory before you take another shot at your goals. Position yourself for success before you take on the challenges of trying to do what other people only dream about doing.

TEAMWORK

The strength of the pack is the wolf,
and the strength of the wolf is the pack.

—Rudyard Kipling

CAPTAIN CHARLES PLUMB was a graduate of the United States Naval Academy. He was a decorated pilot, having flown seventy-four successful combat missions over North Vietnam before he was shot down by enemy anti-aircraft fire. But when the odds caught up with him and his plane was finally brought down, Captain Plumb managed to parachute safely to the ground, where he was captured and held as a prisoner in a small, box-like cell for 2,103 days—almost six years.

After surviving the ordeal, Captain Plumb received the Silver Star, the Bronze Star, the Legion of Merit Award, and two

Purple Hearts. And when he returned to the United States, he frequently spoke to individuals and groups about his experiences in captivity and how they compared to the everyday challenges of life. But shortly after coming home, Charlie and his wife were sitting in a restaurant, where they were approached by a man who was eating at a table nearby.

"You're Plumb," the man said. "You flew jet fighters in Vietnam from the aircraft carrier *Kitty Hawk*. You were shot down."

Surprised at being recognized, Charlie responded, "That's right. But how in the world did you know that?"

The man replied, "I packed your parachute." And as Charlie stared at him in utter disbelief, the man pumped his fist, gave a thumbs-up, and said, "I guess it worked."

Charlie stood to shake the man's hand, assuring him that "it most certainly did work. If it hadn't worked, I wouldn't be here today."

But Charlie couldn't sleep that night, thinking about the man he and his wife had encountered in the restaurant. He wondered what would have happened if the man had not approached him to introduce himself. Charlie would probably have paid no attention to the gentleman across the room, and he probably would have left the restaurant without speaking to him or even knowing the important role that this man had played in his destiny.

Then Charlie wondered how many other people might have played important roles in his life without him even knowing about their contributions. He contemplated how many hours this man must have spent bending over a long wooden table in the hull of an aircraft carrier, carefully folding the silks and weaving the shrouds of each parachute that the ship's pilots would wear into combat, each time holding the fate of those pilots in his hands and each time doing his work behind the scenes, out of sight and out of mind.

With that, Charlie began to realize that a lot more people had contributed to the outcome of his life than he could possibly imagine, because Charlie had needed a lot more in life than just a good parachute. Charlie had needed intellectual training, emotional preparation, and spiritual conditioning to mold him into the man he had turned out to be. During his lifetime, the aging fighter pilot had called upon a vast array of internal and external support systems to bolster him and to sustain him in his times of need. And most of those support systems involved other people, some of them known, but most of them unknown to the man whose life would be shaped by them.

No man is an island. Regardless of how solitary a person may be and regardless of how much a person may pride his individuality and his privacy, we all need each other. And more people contribute to our lives and to the outcome of our lives than we care to admit. This is why teamwork is so important. This is why the truly successful and the truly great achievers in life learn to appreciate the value that other people add to them. They draw upon the resources of others, but, at the same time, they make their own talents and resources available to others who are attempting their own great feats in life.

This is especially true in athletic competition. Athletic competition depends on the individual achievements of its participants, but the individual achievements of athletes depend on teamwork. Obviously, there are two major categories of sports: individual sports like bowling, archery, and golf and team sports like baseball, basketball, and football. But even in those sports where athletes compete as individuals, there is always a team of people involved in those athletes' success. There are coaches, trainers, promoters, nutritionists, agents, caddies, and managers surrounding that athlete in an effort to help him achieve his full potential in his sport. No one achieves anything notable or worthwhile—in athletics or in life—without the direct and indirect involvement of other people.

Basketball, particularly, is a sport where individual players can shine and where individual performances can rouse the emotions of the crowd. But a basketball star never gains stardom by working alone. Behind every Michael Jordan and every LeBron James are parents who encouraged them, high school coaches who recognized their potential, college coaches who helped them perfect their craft, and a host of friends and teammates who created an atmosphere where their skills could be utilized and their talents could be displayed.

MOST VALUABLE PLAYER

Earvin "Magic" Johnson was a particularly gifted basketball player, yet he was well aware that his personal success was due largely to the contribution of his teammates and the staff around him.

According to Pat Riley, the head coach of the Los Angeles Lakers during Magic Johnson's stellar career with that team, Magic was a very gifted player, even as a youth. In high school, he led his team to the state championship and he twice won All-State honors. And during his brief college career, Magic continued to add championships to his résumé, leading his Michigan State Spartans to the NCAA title before being drafted by the Lakers. Then, in his first year in the NBA, he was named Rookie of the Year, and, once more, he led a talented team to the championship. But after winning the title that year, Coach Riley told Magic that he had never seen anyone quite like him in more than twenty years as a player and a coach. He had never seen anyone who worked so hard to combine great talent with a great attitude.

That's when Coach Riley asked Magic how he came to be that way, and Magic told him that over the course of his career, as his teams were winning one championship after another, he would look around for opportunities to share his joy with his victorious teammates. But the other players never seemed to feel the same way that Magic felt about the team's achievements. They seemed strangely unhappy, even in the aftermath of great victories.

But Magic told Coach Riley that he soon figured out what was wrong. He was always the one handling the ball and taking the shots, especially the important shots, because his coaches had told him that he was the biggest and the best player on the court and that he should dominate the game for the sake of his team. But by doing so, his teammates were made to feel like "nobodies," and that made Magic Johnson miserable.

So Magic eventually came to realize that it was more important to share success with those who had helped him achieve success than it was to win a multitude of individual awards. And this lesson, obtained during his youth, helped shape Magic's attitude, making him one of the best team players in the history of professional basketball.

While under contract with the Lakers, Magic Johnson became renowned for his unselfish play and for making his teammates better by refusing to function apart from them. And as the team connected and started working together as "one," they reaped the benefits of their unparalleled teamwork. They won five NBA championships, and Magic Johnson was named Most Valuable Player three times.

Pat Riley, who coached four of those championship teams, wrote, "My driving belief is this: Great teamwork is the only way to reach our ultimate moments, to create breakthroughs that define our careers, to fulfill our lives with a sense of lasting significance."

So teamwork in basketball is extremely important, because teams simply do not win without it. Even though the evening highlight reels always show the dazzling shots and the thunderous dunks of individual performers, it is the combined efforts of a synchronized team that consistently scores points and successfully keeps the other teams at bay. And ironically, it is often the greatest individual performers who are the first to recognize the importance of the other members of the team and the necessity of their contribution.

Michael Jordan, perhaps the greatest player in the history of the game, said, "Talent wins games, but teamwork and intelligence win championships." And John Wooden, the winningest coach in college basketball history, said, "The main ingredient of stardom is the rest of the team."

Although a lot of individual qualities are needed to succeed and to bounce back from past failures, most of life's achievements are reserved for a team of people. Sometimes those people know that they are a team, and sometimes they simply function as a team by virtue of their synergy and interaction. Thomas Edison, for instance, got all the credit for inventing the phonograph, the camera, and the light bulb. But "Thomas Edison" was actually a team of people, not an isolated individual wearing a white coat in his laboratory in Menlo Park.

So before you attempt another shot at the things that matter most to you in life, stop for a few moments and take a quick assessment of the role that teamwork might play in your future success and how the absence of teamwork may have contributed to your past failures. Ask yourself these questions:

- Did you fail because of a lack of talent, or did you fail because of a lack of connections?

- Did you fail because of a lack of effort, or did you fail because of a lack of coordination with other people?

- Were your efforts lacking because there were some pieces missing from your puzzle?

- Were your victories few and your setbacks many because you were performing alone and there was no one to help you when you needed help the most?

Almost everything in life is a team effort. Obviously, your portion of the effort depends on your own knowledge and persistence and timing and strength. Unless you master your own qualities of greatness and position yourself to do your part of the equation, success will always elude you. But even if you do more than your share with absolute precision and perfection, you will still fall short of the mark unless you have the backing of a team of people who support you in your efforts. In sports, you need coaches, trainers, and other players who can do the things you cannot do. In business, you need accountants, attorneys, and laborers who are gifted at the things you find difficult. In life, you need colleagues who will tell you the truth, mentors who will guide you reliably, and friends who will stand by you on both the days of triumph and the days of tragedy.

GEESE IN FLIGHT

Sompong Yusoontorn is a motivational instructor who often shares captivating insights about leadership, success, and other qualities people want to pursue in their lives. In one of his lessons, Yusoontorn offers an intriguing comparison between migratory birds and human beings, showing various ways in which the survival of the flock is comparable to the survival of people in threatening situations. Yusoontorn says there are several principles we can learn about teamwork by watching geese and other migratory birds in flight.

Teamwork is uplifting. Migratory birds fly in formation to create lift for the entire flock. The bird flying in the lead position works especially hard to create an environment for the other birds that lightens their load and makes it possible for them to travel thousands of miles in a matter of a few days. But when the lead bird tires, another bird assumes his position as he falls back with the others. And with the help of this illustration from nature, we can better understand the important role of other people in the achievement of our goals. Just as the birds take turns flying at the head of the flock, we must also lead sometimes and follow sometimes. It is never a bad idea to follow people who are going where we want to go, and it is always a good idea to share the workload along the way.

Teamwork benefits the individual. Whenever a migratory bird falls out of formation, he immediately feels the increased workload of flying alone, because the drag created by his isolation takes a toll on his energy. He soon realizes that he is not taking advantage of the lift created by the flock, and he will hurry to reestablish his position in the formation. Working collectively benefits us individually. If we hope to safely arrive at our destination, we must be willing to both give help and to seek help from those who are traveling where we want to go.

Teamwork involves trust. Some tasks are just downright difficult. In the same way that the lead bird will occasionally drop back in the formation so he can let another bird take his turn in front of the flock, you must learn to delegate tasks and authority. Surround yourself with trustworthy people; then have confidence in their abilities. When you learn to rely on the vast resources that have been placed at your disposal in the form of the people around you, you will find that the struggles become easier and the load becomes much lighter.

Teamwork provides encouragement. Have you ever noticed how a flock of geese tend to honk as they fly by? You might think this unwise, because the excessive honking should tire the geese more quickly. But the honking is an intentional part of their nature. The geese flying in formation honk because they want to encourage the lone bird at the head of the flock to keep up his good work. They want to push him forward while reminding him they are relying on his good efforts and they have his back. So while the lead bird uses all his energy to create uplift for the rest of the flock, the birds flying in formation use their energy to encourage the lead bird. This is the way it should be in your life, too. You should always encourage those who are carrying a heavy load, and you should show gratitude and respect to them for what they contribute to your life. And when it is your turn to take the lead, you should expect others to do the same for you. If those around you are always taking *from* you without contributing *to* your life, that may be one of the causes for your past failures. You need to create and nurture relationships that are beneficial and balanced in their requirements and benefits.

Teamwork offers support. Occasionally a bird gets sick or injured and has to abandon the journey. And when he does, one or two of the healthy birds will go down to the ground with him to help protect him and care for him. As you take another shot at your dreams, you will have some good days and some bad days. You will have some victories and some defeats. So learn to stand by the significant people in your life when they need your help, and learn to draw from others in your own times of need. An attitude of going it alone and doing everything by yourself may be an exciting plot for a Hollywood movie, but it is a lousy plot for real life, a plot that can lead to burnout and failure, isolation and loneliness. There are a lot of ups and downs along life's way. So if you don't have the help and support of others, you won't get very far. Besides, even if you should defy the odds and arrive at your destination alone, what kind of joy would you find there if you had no one to share it with?

Moving forward then, determine that you are going to do two things as you prepare to take another shot at your dream. First, determine that you are going to learn how to be a team player. Being a team player means giving of yourself, and that won't come naturally. If you want a vital and essential team around you, you are going to have to learn to encourage, to share, to trust, and to support others before you can expect them to trust and support you. So do what it takes to get the ball rolling. Step up and be a contributing part of a whole that benefits everyone involved. Make your abilities available to other people while you draw upon the wisdom and resources of others in those areas where you are weak, inexperienced, or lacking. Learn to be a team player.

Second, build your own team. Determine that you will work hard to surround yourself with the kind of people who can propel you to greatness, people who can challenge you to think great things, motivate you to believe in yourself, and help you to do what is necessary to get where you want to go. Build a network of people around you who can nurture all the important aspects of your life, from your spirituality to your professional pursuits. Pour yourself into those relationships that help you fulfill your purpose, but minimize or eliminate those relationships that detract you from noble things. More than you realize, you become the company that you keep.

There is a lot of wisdom in the old adage, "Show me your friends, and I'll show you your future." And as motivational speaker Jim Rohn is so fond of saying, "You are the average of the five people you spend the most time with." So I cannot stress enough the importance of the people you choose as your teammates. You need to know who is adding to your life and who is subtracting from it. And you need to know the difference between the person who is temporarily in need of your help and the person who perpetually drains you and your resources. So pick the members of your team with great care and great caution, and work hard to build a supportive network of friends and associates who can benefit your life, because the people around you will either contribute to you or detract from you. They will either sustain you or destroy you.

In the Northern Hemisphere, migratory birds fly south for the winter. Even the animals know their destination when they reach it, so they don't continue to fly forever. You, too, need definable goals. You need to know where you are in your journey, and you need to know when you have arrived at your destination. And when you do finally arrive, you need to take a break and share the rewards of your hard work with those who helped you get there. Whether your teammates are obvious to you (like employees and partners) or concealed from your view (like the guy who folded parachutes on the *Kitty Hawk*), they are critical to your success.

You cannot make it alone, no matter how hard you try. Winning requires teamwork, and good teamwork requires a winning team.

TECHNIQUE

The Results of Practice
and Hard Work

STRENGTH

I want you to be forever strong on the field
so you will be forever strong off it.

—Larry Gelwix

THE GROUND around El shimmered with intense heat. In the valley below, he could see the angry men rushing toward him and could hear the heavy clanking of swords against armor. He stood still. And as the enemy soldiers grew closer, El saw the intense hatred on their faces and heard their snarling curses. Yet he refused to budge.

Just a few minutes earlier, El had been surrounded by his fellow soldiers, but now he was standing alone. When his friends had noticed the approaching danger, they ran away, intimidated by the sheer numbers of the enemy and frightened by the thought that death might come that day.

"Let's wait," they urged, fear choking their voices. "There will be another time."

But El knew it would not matter. Another day! Another month! How long could they survive? They were outnumbered and surrounded. Their families were constantly threatened, and their land had been plundered. There would be no negotiations. No mercy! No assistance! This enemy had killed before, and they would kill again. The only thing these people understood was strength, and the only way to stop them was through brute force. So El stood alone, ready to do battle. And the enemy attacked.

From behind the rocks on an adjoining hill, the deserters watched the assault. The fighting was vicious, even though it was just one man against a horde of sadistic killers. So what chance did he have? They knew El would soon be dead. Yet they watched anyway. In fact, they had to watch. After all, he was one of them. He was strong, he was brave, and he was a respected leader among them. But now he would die. And for what? What would change?

Was there any point in fighting? El thought so. He had told the others time and time again that there would come a day when they would have to make a stand. He said that strength was their only hope and that, at all costs, this enemy must not be allowed to prevail. So they looked on, and they waited for the tragic outcome that they knew was inevitable.

El swung his sword ferociously, lunging viciously at the brutal attackers. He lost all track of time and his vision narrowed to the immediate battle, each thrust, each parry. His sword became an extension of his arm as he fought for his life. And soon the ground around El became littered with the fallen corpses of enemy soldiers, yet the soldiers continued to come and El continued to fight. His great strength became his means of survival and El battled on, turning to meet yet another attack from behind. The sound of clashing metal echoed through the valley along with the screams of the stricken soldiers and El's own maniacal battle cries.

Meanwhile, the soldiers behind the rocks watched in utter amazement. El was still standing. It was impossible, but he was still fighting, and he was winning. All alone, one strong man was prevailing against this company of evil adversaries. The other soldiers couldn't quite believe it, but this was actually happening, and it was happening before their very eyes.

"Let's GO!" someone finally shouted, and they returned together to join the fight. But by the time they crossed the valley and reached the scene of the battle, all was quiet. El stood alone, just as he had when they left him. All around him was the carnage from the fight. There was not an enemy soldier left standing.

El saw the men returning to his side, and as they arrived on that sacred hill, he tried to put down his sword to make contact with them. But he could not loosen his grip. Because he had fought so intensely and for such a long time, his muscles were frozen in place and he could not release his weapon. So he stood there before them, a warrior and a victor, with his sword in his hand. And all that remained was to strip the dead, checking for weapons and for anything useful.

You may recognize the hero of this story—El or Eleazar—because he was one of King David's "mighty men." These exceptional men had been handpicked by David because of their courage, their loyalty, their unflinching determination, and their legendary strength, and they were a fascinating company of brave warriors. So when you need some inspiration from some real-life heroes, try reading about the "mighty men" of David. You can find their stories in II Samuel 8 and I Chronicles 11.

But the thing you need to know right now as you consider another shot at your dreams is that although David's mighty men have been dead for more than 3,000 years, the qualities that made these men so great are the same qualities that give rise to greatness in our lives: courage, loyalty, determination, and strength. In this chapter, therefore, I want to explore the quality of strength, because, no matter who you are—male or female, businessman or athlete, rookie or veteran—you need strength. To succeed in life and especially to take another shot after a crushing defeat requires mental and physical toughness.

So I want to look at three areas where strength will be required in your journey back to the top. I want to show you how you will need strength of purpose, strength of endurance, and strength of performance if you intend to succeed in your efforts to achieve success. Then later in this chapter, we will consider the importance of physical strength and the value inherent in recognizing your own strengths, as well as your weaknesses.

STRENGTH OF PURPOSE

Basketball is a very physical game. Many people mistakenly believe that basketball is a gentle sport. In reality, however, basketball is like football or hockey: it is a sport that can take a heavy toll on a player's body. Particularly beneath the basket, the game gets extremely physical. Players are constantly pushing one another with their arms, legs, and torsos to get in position to score or to get in position to rebound the ball when another player misses his shot.

But a great basketball player needs more than just physical strength; a great basketball player needs strength of purpose, as well. He needs to know what he wants to do, and then he needs to dispense with the excuses and do it.

Obviously, strength of purpose functions on many levels in the game of basketball. When a player takes the court, for instance, he must have a clear understanding of his purpose in the game. But on a more elemental level (the micro level), he must have a clear sense of purpose each trip down the court. He must make each move count if he plans to achieve his goal during that possession. In addition, a great ball player must have a large-scale (macro) view of his purpose. His purpose should be bigger than just this one game. He should have goals for the season, and he should have goals for his career.

Tiger Woods, for example, has boldly announced his primary

career goal in the world of professional golf. Obviously, he has a game plan in mind every time he approaches the first tee of a tournament. And obviously, he has a particular plan in mind for each hole that he plays and for each individual shot that he makes during a round. But Tiger Woods has a bigger plan for his career than simply making par on that difficult dogleg par-4 or simply winning the Masters or the PGA Championship. Tiger Woods wants to break Jack Nicklaus' lifetime record of eighteen major championships, and Tiger currently has fourteen of those titles to his credit.

And similar to Tiger Woods' purpose for how he intends to play each shot, each hole, and each tournament and how he intends to approach his career, you should have an overarching purpose for every important aspect of your life. You should have a comprehensive purpose for your life, too. But it's not enough to declare a long-term purpose for your life without making that purpose the driving force behind everything you do each day. On your journey to greatness, the main thing is that you keep the main thing the main thing.

I can't tell you, for instance, how many times someone has told me that he is planning to write a book or that publishing his own book is one of his primary goals in life. And frankly, I think this kind of goal is commendable, because being an author is a noble ambition. But when I ask these would-be writers what they are doing each day to make this dream a reality in their lives, I usually get evasive answers that are designed to change the subject. Some of them say they have written down a few ideas, but most of them have nothing more than a vague concept for a book in their heads. They haven't even developed an outline.

Very few wannabe authors are actually working each day to publish the books they say they want to write. They aren't actually typing, nor are they making notes or conducting research. They aren't investigating publishers, nor are they determining the best ways to market their manuscripts or to procure the services of a literary agent. They aren't willing to do the work that is necessary to actually turn their ideas into 64,000 words of polished prose, because they aren't really serious about doing what they say they want to do. They aren't willing to do the work that is necessary to be an author, because writing a book is not really the all-consuming motivation of their lives that they profess it to be.

So it is vital to define your goals, but you can only define your specific goals when you understand the overall purpose of your life. A comprehensive purpose helps a person define what he wants to do with his life, and more importantly, what he doesn't want to do. So if a person's comprehensive plan is to build a thriving business or to find a cure for pancreatic cancer, that person probably will never write a book. Instead, books will be written about him. But if that person's comprehensive plan is to actually write material that can benefit people in specific areas of their lives, he won't stop with one rejection letter from a potential publisher and he won't stop with one denial from a literary agent. He will write his first book anyway, and he will promote his book even if it takes him twenty years to get it published.

So write down your "macro" goal, and put it somewhere so you can read it every day. By making the primary purpose of your life the centerpiece of all your thinking, you can keep yourself focused on the bigger picture of your life, which can help you make good decisions regarding all the little things that are destined to consume your time and define your legacy. A constant reminder of your life's purpose can also give you a clearer perspective on life in the face of victory, as well as occasional defeat.

If you don't know your purpose in life, you won't have the necessary focus to prevail. And if you don't have the focus needed to prevail in life's battles, you certainly won't have the resolve to bounce back from a disappointing performance. So define your purpose in life, because you need the kind of strength that can only flow from strength of purpose.

STRENGTH OF ENDURANCE

Great athletes also possess strength of endurance. They have the "wind" to give it everything they've got for as long as it takes. Yes, physical strength is important and strength of purpose is necessary, too, if a competitive person hopes to prevail over his opposition. But in every sport, as in life, the ability to endure is just as important, because the game lasts a long time and weariness becomes a huge factor in defeat.

For example, a professional basketball game consists of four quarters, each quarter consisting of 12 minutes of active play. And the players never stop moving during those 48 minutes when the clock is running. So the players on the court are constantly jumping, stopping, sprinting, and changing directions as they attempt to score points and keep the opposing team from scoring points. Therefore, without strong lungs and a strong heart, basketball players could not compete and they certainly could not win.

So professional athletes spend an enormous amount of time conditioning not only their muscles, but their lungs, as well. They run sprints. They run long distances. They run up and down stairs until they are completely exhausted ... and then they run up and down some more stairs. They do a lot of intense cardiovascular training to build their stamina while they build their strength and hone their skills.

You should do the same thing. You should develop the strength to go the distance. As with basketball, life isn't about a single shot; it's about the bigger picture of the game itself. A lot of teams come out on the court red hot, running up big numbers early in the game. But unless those teams can maintain that kind of momentum for 48 continuous minutes of hard play, they usually end up losing. In fact, I've seen it happen many times. I've seen teams run up a 24-point lead early in the game only to lose that lead and lose the game because they lacked the endurance to go the distance.

Strength of endurance seems to be the focus of many athletes right now—how to be stronger, longer. And the same focus should consume anyone who is competing for a worthy prize. In the end, the outcome of your life, like the outcome of an athletic event, will be determined partly by how fit you are to compete, but mostly by how long you are able to stay in the game. Because a lifetime goal cannot be achieved quickly, you must have the staying power that is necessary to outlast your competition, and you must be patient as you commit yourself to the long-term pursuit of your dreams.

You cannot count on your talents alone. You cannot count solely on your skills or your experience. Certainly these things are important, and they can definitely give you an advantage over a less skillful or less experienced competitor. But in the end, the person with endurance will likely prevail. The person with endurance will even prevail over someone with noticeably greater abilities, because the prize goes to the tortoise who can see the race through to the end, not to the hare who can dazzle the crowd with one or two amazing bursts of speed.

STRENGTH OF PERFORMANCE

Finally, great athletes demonstrate strength of performance. They execute on the field of play.

In the United States, people are judged primarily by what they do, not by what they think they can do or what they say they can do. Our culture respects and rewards performance. We are impressed by people who can actually do what they set out to do.

In fact, we can see this focus on performance every day. Every day, you hear about actors who have signed big contracts to make high-budget movies, and you wonder if those actors can really sell the tickets they claim they can sell. You hear about athletes who have signed multimillion-dollar contracts, and you wonder if those athletes can really live up to their billing. Some prove to be worth their weight in gold, and some even transcend what is expected of them, driving up their value the next time they find themselves negotiating a contract. But you also have seen those athletes who talk loud and perform with a whimper, and you have seen those politicians who promise the moon and leave us suffering with buyer's remorse.

In this country and in most Western cultures, we are impressed by one thing and one thing alone: performance. When push comes to shove, it's not about the traditions, it's not about the stadium or the cheerleaders, and it's not about the commercial endorsements or the pre-game hype. No matter how many analysts try to predict the outcome of a game, the real question is which team will perform best when the athletes finally suit up and take the field, because the championship trophy will be presented to the team that scores the most points, not the team that has the coolest uniforms, the best statistics, or the highest-paid athletes.

So you must be prepared to perform. Your business cards may be the best in your profession. Your family's reputation may be respected throughout the region. Your ideas may be exciting, and your friends may be too numerous to count. But until you actually do what you say you are going to do, you are merely a rookie without a résumé. So stop talking about what you are going to do and stop pointing at what your father and grandfather did before you, and just do what you say you are going to do.

"You gain strength, courage, and confidence by each experience in which you really stop to look fear in the face," said Eleanor Roosevelt. "You must do the thing you think you cannot do." And that is why strength is essential in your personal efforts to rebound from your past mistakes and failures. If you have failed one or more times in the past, the fear can be pretty daunting because nobody wants to fail a second or third time. But as you confront the challenge of taking another shot at your dreams, strength will give you what you need to overcome your trepidation, and strength will give you what you need to follow through.

ARE YOU STRONG ENOUGH?

Some people cannot play basketball because they don't have the physical attributes to compete with those who do. They lack either the height or the speed or the strength that is necessary to contend with the other players. Similarly, there are certain qualities that a person needs before going up against the forces that stand between him and his goals. So a smart person will honestly evaluate his potential for success before he attempts to do something he may not be equipped to do.

Now please understand, I am not saying that you may be incapable of achieving your dreams. If a person has a burning desire that will not fade away and if that person is willing to do the necessary work and pay the necessary price to give life to his desires, he can accomplish just about anything he puts his mind to. But I also believe that a legitimate dream is a never-ending process. It is an unfolding pursuit, not a flashing thought or a single act. So the person who has a viable dream in his heart will meditate on that dream, visualize that dream, and talk about that dream to anyone who will listen. He will research ways to fulfill his dream and brainstorm his ideas with other people who have already done what he wants to do. He will spend months and years plotting his course and then additional time "working" his dream in order to make it happen in his lifetime.

The achievement of a personal vision is not a fly-by-night or flash-in-the-pan experience; it is a journey, a lengthy journey. And somewhere along the way, the person with a dream will need to honestly ask himself whether he has the talents, the skills, and the attributes necessary to achieve success. Honest, gut-wrenching self-evaluation is part of the process of giving life to an unfolding pursuit.

But because the experiences of life will force us to scrutinize ourselves and evaluate our own limitations, some people will discover from their encounters that they should modify their dreams to match up with their talents. They will learn that the full discovery of one's destiny occurs, not in a moment of inspiration, but in those sometimes difficult situations where our hopes and dreams merge with the cold, hard facts of life. Where objective truth intersects with internal ambition, there one will find his calling.

So if you have taken shots in the past and have missed them and if you are thinking about taking another shot at your dreams, you need to ask yourself if you have what it takes to be successful at the thing you are trying to do. And if you don't have what it takes, you need to ask yourself if you can develop those necessary qualities before you inject yourself back into that ruthless, painful game that has already sidelined you at least once.

If you want to be a successful entrepreneur, you must possess certain qualities that can equip you for success in the business arena. You must be decisive, you must be flexible, and you must exhibit traits of leadership. If you want to be a successful politician, you must possess certain personal qualities that can equip you for success in the world of public service. You must be able to speak in front of large crowds, you must be able to relate to people from all levels of society, and you must be able to negotiate. If you want to be a schoolteacher or a minister or an engineer or an entertainer, you must possess the corresponding strengths that are necessary for success in those particular fields. Whatever you want to do with your life, you must bring certain strengths to the table if you hope to succeed. If you don't have those particular strengths, you need to obtain them or consider another course.

Somewhere along the way, short basketball players figure out that they cannot be great rebounders; nevertheless, they can still lead the league in three-point shooting. And taller players eventually learn that they cannot run the offense while dribbling the ball; nevertheless, they can still make it to the Hall of Fame as inside scorers and rebounders. So part of the process of achievement is discovering your own inadequacies so you can either overcome those inadequacies or learn to work around them. I believe that God gives every person a pretty equitable balance of strengths and limitations. He gave us strengths so we could achieve our created purpose in life, but he gave us limitations to keep us humble, to keep us dependent on him and others, and to help us focus on the thing we ought to be doing instead of allowing ourselves to be distracted by the constant emergence of unrealistic fantasies.

Life is filled with competition and life is filled with conflict, whether we like those things or not. And there is nothing wrong with that, because competition is not immoral. In fact, competition is the essence of life. Competition in life is born out of the conflict that naturally arises when two people chase the same prize, just as competition on the basketball court is born out of the conflict that naturally arises when two players chase the same ball.

So competition is essential in sports just as competition is essential in business. Competition is essential in sports just as competition is essential in romance, in academics, and in every other worthwhile pursuit in life. It isn't wise, therefore, to think of one person as being right and the other person as being wrong whenever conflict arises. Life just isn't that simplistic. Rather, competition is the natural outflow of two people chasing the same dream or two people chasing different dreams that carry them down convergent paths. Competition is what happens when two good businessmen pursue the same customer.

But this competitive nature of life is the reason you need strength. A great athlete, particularly a great basketball player, needs to be physically strong if he hopes to compete and win.

And you need to be strong in order to compete, as well. In fact, the physical requirements of the game of basketball demand that a player be strong. He must have strong arms and muscular legs before he ever takes the court. And if you will pay close attention the next time you watch a game on television, you will notice that all the great players, particularly the great inside players, have enormous biceps and broad shoulders. They bring brute force to the game before the ball is even tipped.

But what you cannot grasp just by watching a game is that these men work hard during the off season to build their strength because they know that their raw physical power is one of the most vital assets they possess. So these great players work year-around to build muscle mass, they eat diets specifically crafted for them by professional nutritionists, and they work daily with personal trainers so they can enhance their God-given power.

Similarly, you must be physically and emotionally built for your chosen pursuits if you hope to rebound from past failures and compete for your dreams. God has given you certain strengths and talents that are designed to help you succeed in your chosen field of competition. If you have missed shots in the past, therefore, those missed shots can probably be traced back to your lack of attention to the strengths God gave to you. Like a lot of basketball players, you may have stopped nurturing your strengths in order to put more emphasis on overcoming your weaknesses. But as legendary football coach Paul "Bear" Bryant once said, "You win games with your strengths, not your weaknesses."

So focusing on improving your weaknesses rather than your strengths is a formula for failure. Great rebounders don't spend time trying to learn to dribble the basketball, and great ball handlers don't spend time trying to learn to position themselves for rebounds. Successful athletes focus on their strengths, learning to maximize what they do better than anyone else. They leave it to others to do what they lack the talent to do. And you need to follow in their footsteps. If a vision burns within your heart, you probably have the talents you need to realize that vision. But you won't achieve your dream if you neglect the talents that gave rise to your potential in order to improve skills that have nothing to do with your destiny.

So ask yourself: What are my natural talents and abilities? Do they match up with what I want to do? If so, how can I improve them and strengthen them? If not, how can I make adjustments so my goals align with the realities of who I am? A great rebounder needs physical strength if he hopes to prevail on the backboards, and a great ball handler needs speed if he hopes to manage his team's offense. Likewise, a person needs natural strengths if he hopes to prevail in life.

Quoting Rev. Phillips Brooks at a presidential prayer breakfast in 1963, John F. Kennedy told the nation, "Do not pray for easy lives. Pray to be stronger men." Resistance makes you grow strong. So do not pray for lower goals or easier shots or weaker opponents or the disqualification of your competitors. Instead, prepare yourself to meet life's challenges head-on and, like Eleazar, a leader among King David's mighty men, prepare yourself to do battle even if you must stand alone when the fighting is its fiercest.

BALANCE

It's not the load that breaks you down;
it's the way you carry it.
—Lou Holtz

I DON'T PLAY GOLF, but I was recently talking with a friend of mine who does play. He lives here in Central Florida, and he was sharing some of the challenges he faces when he plays golf in our subtropical weather during the summer months. If you have never lived in Florida, you might not be aware that it rains every day here during the summer months. Every afternoon, rain showers sweep across the state, almost at precisely the same time each day.

In addition to dodging rain showers, another issue my friend has been encountering lately is strong, gusty winds. As the storms move into the area and then pass quickly through, they are preceded by strong winds. And my friend was telling me that, while he can manage playing in the rain, he cannot seem to manage the wind. The wind blows his golf ball all over the place, and the wind blows dirt and sand back in his face every time he hits the ball.

But worst of all, the wind causes him to lose his balance. A great golf swing is a precise mechanical operation. Actually, it is a series of precise mechanical operations, and there is little room for error. A sudden gust of wind or a substantial sustained breeze can make it virtually impossible for a golfer to keep his balance while he is going through the motions of his swing.

So my friend was telling me how this increase in wind velocity affects his game. As the storm clouds roll through the area, even though they may not drop any rain on the golf course, the winds that whip up ahead of the clouds always seem to ruin his game. While he typically shoots par or bogey on most holes, he considers himself fortunate to get a double bogey when the winds are swirling.

Balance is important in golf. In fact, balance is important in most sports. Balance is one of the fundamental prerequisites for success in such sports as bowling, archery, skiing, hockey, boxing, and target shooting. In these and other sports like them, where movement is constant and sometimes dramatic or where absolute control of one's motions is critical, balance is the key to performance.

Balance is essential in basketball, too. In fact, perfect balance is vital in the game of basketball. It is impossible to shoot effectively if you aren't balanced when you take your shot. It is impossible to pull down a rebound and then feed the ball down court for a fast break if you lose your balance when you come down with the ball. It is impossible to defend a great scorer or to keep him from taking open shots if you cannot keep your balance while moving your feet.

In fact, the great scorers in basketball excel at throwing their defenders off balance. A great shooting guard, for instance, will often receive a pass at the top of the "key" and then stand there with the ball, faking movements with his body and his eyes until his defender finally falls for one of his deceptions, and then, while the defender is momentarily off balance, the shooting guard will take advantage of the situation by driving to the basket.

In the same way that balance is important to a shooter and a defender, balance is important to a rebounder, as well. If a rebounder jumps high and comes down with the basketball, his success will be short lived if he loses his balance before he regains his footing. Many a big man has snatched a rebound off the backboard only to take a step when landing on the floor. And many a player has been charged with a foul for placing his hand on an opposing player to steady himself while jumping. So balance is essential throughout the game of basketball, and perhaps that is why a number of NBA teams have hired full-time balance coaches to help their players develop the coordination they need to maintain their stability on the court.

But balance is vital in other ways, as well. Not only do individual players need to develop balance in order to properly execute the mechanics of the game; the team also needs balance in order to win consistently. A good basketball team has to have balance between size and speed, between offense and defense, and between strength and endurance.

Just think about it! Many people believe that height is the only thing that counts in the game of basketball. But a team consisting of five extremely tall players could never win consistently in a competitive league because the athletes on that team would be slower than a team consisting of five shorter players, and those five shorter players would eventually find a way to exhaust the big men and defeat them. Likewise, most people believe that defense is the key to winning basketball games, particularly at the college level. But even the best defensive team cannot win on a consistent basis if that team is incapable of scoring when they take possession of the ball.

A good player—in basketball and in every other sport—is a player who has developed physical balance for the sport he plays and balance in the skills the game requires of him. And a good team—in basketball and in every other sport—is a team that has developed balance in its strategy and balance in its execution of the elements of the game. Without balance, the other ingredients of success, like strength and aggressiveness, cannot yield reliable results for a player and cannot produce a winning season for a team.

Balance is one of those vital qualities that determine the outcome of most sporting events and the outcome of life itself. In fact, without balance a person can still do some truly remarkable things in competition and in life through the sheer force of his determination. But with a sense of balance, a person can do the things that he does more consistently, more efficiently, and with more impressive results. Balance, therefore, is the invisible attribute that makes all your other attributes work together to achieve their God-given purpose.

But to have true balance in your life, you need to have a clear understanding of what balance really is. Too often, we adopt false expectations of life and unrealistic expectations of ourselves that put pressure on us to try to do too many things with our limited time and resources. We start looking around and begin noticing what other people are doing with their lives, and we tend to think that we are supposed to do all the things that those other people are doing while balancing all the same activities adeptly. These absurd comparisons then lead us to ask ourselves some pretty self-defeating questions: How can others manage to stay balanced, but I can't? How do other people manage to have such perfect families and such rewarding careers when I can barely keep my head above water? Why are others asked to serve as leaders in their churches and communities when nobody even notices leadership potential in me?

Questions like this, stemming from unwise comparisons and inaccurate observations, create guilt, self-recrimination, and a feeling of inadequacy in a person's life because the person asking these questions fails to understand what real balance looks like in everyday life. Instead of having a healthy view of balance, a person with this mindset has an idealistic expectation of life that is destined to breed disappointment.

So first, let me tell you to stop comparing yourself to others. Many times, the lives of those we admire from afar are not at all what we think they are. Many times, these people are concealing the struggles they have in life while accentuating their victories. But even if some of these people should have their lives together in every conceivable way, what is that to you and your goals in life? You need to stop putting yourself down by constantly comparing yourself to a fabricated image that you cannot possibly satisfy. Instead, let me show you what I believe a balanced life really look like.

Imagine this. You are strolling through the city one afternoon, and up ahead you notice a street performer. He is juggling a bunch of brightly colored balls, and he seems quite adept at keeping all of the balls in the air at the same time. So as you step aside to watch the show, you decide to take some pictures of this seemingly impressive event. But later, when you start sorting the pictures and cropping them, you begin noticing that there's a method behind the madness of juggling balls. In one picture, a blue ball is on top of the juggler's circle. In another picture, a red ball is on top of the arc. And in yet another photo, you notice an orange ball at the apex of the juggler's circle. And then you realize that at no moment in time were all the balls on top of the arc or at the bottom of the arc. They were constantly changing positions. But none of the balls were ever on the ground, either.

I believe this is a great illustration of what real balance should look like in a person's life. We are constantly juggling "balls" in our lives, those areas of concern that we must keep in motion and which demand our constant attention. Your balls, for instance, may include work, school, your spouse, your children, your spiritual life, friends, hobbies, church attendance, and other things. Every day your balls are moving, constantly changing position and constantly fluctuating in importance and relevance. But the key to successfully juggling all your balls is to simply avoid dropping any of them.

Remember the pictures you took of the juggler? At any particular moment in time, any of the juggler's balls could have been at the top of his circle and any of them could have been at the bottom. However, the many balls he was juggling could never have been at the top of the arc all at the same time. Instead, they rotated from top to bottom and from hand-to-hand, giving each of them an equal amount of attention over time. Similarly, your life is a lot like the juggler's technique. At any given moment, one of your balls might need more attention than the others. This is normal. But balance is needed in your life if you want to make sure one ball does not stay on the top of your arc too long to the detriment of your other balls. If you are only highlighting one area of your life all the time, the other important aspects of your life will suffer.

So this might be a good time to reassess those areas of your life that are constantly vying for your attention. Are all of them important? Sometimes, the best way to keep all your balls in the air is to reduce the number of balls you are trying to juggle. For instance, if you are trying to manage your home, your continuing education, aging parents, the needs of your children, your job, a homeless ministry at your church, and a new business you are trying to launch while simultaneously working to strengthen your spiritual life, you might want to take a closer look at the obligations you have piled upon yourself. And when you do, you may need to reprioritize your life and then postpone or eliminate some of the things on your list. But be honest. You want to simplify so you can focus and balance. Even the best jugglers will drop their balls if they try to handle too many.

Fortunately, the degree of balance you have in your life will often manifest itself in your demeanor and may affect the way others view you. So a good question to ask yourself while you are taking inventory of your responsibilities is, "What characterizes my life?" You also may want to ask some of your friends and family members to describe your demeanor in one word, because their objective analysis of your approach to life can give you additional insight into how balanced or unbalanced your life really is. Do your friends describe you as stressed? Always running? Frequently late? Frustrated and angry? Or do they describe you as calm? Patient? Confident? In control? Get an accurate snapshot of your own life and the balls you are trying to juggle, and let that understanding guide you in selecting how many balls you think can actually handle without dropping any.

Then, when you have all the right balls in your hands and you are ready to start juggling again, remember that different balls will reach the zenith of your circle at different times. Each ball will be on top of the circle at some point in time, but the balls cannot all be at the top of the circle at the same time. So look at your life from a realistic perspective and see if the balls you are juggling are all receiving their due attention. Balance is achieved by living your life without dropping any of your balls.

If you have failed in the past, perhaps you ought to take a closer look at your sense of balance, and perhaps you should give some consideration to developing better balance in your life. Specifically, there are three areas where you must develop balance if you intend to succeed in the future where you have failed in the past. You must have a balance of priorities, a balance of sacrifice, and a balance of expectations.

A BALANCE OF PRIORITIES

What are your priorities in life? Obviously, different things are important to different people. And even among those people who share the same values, their individual lists may reflect a different order for their shared priorities. But generally speaking, I believe that three things in life matter most. When all is said and done and when a person is taking inventory of his life, he will probably agree on the priority of these three areas: his spiritual life, his meaningful relationships, and his personal destiny and legacy. At the end of his time on earth, a person will know that he has been successful if these three dimensions of his life have given him a sense of fulfillment. But if he finds himself lacking in one or more of these vital aspects of life or if he has neglected one or more of them completely, he will find a deep void in his life that will bring him great sorrow and perhaps some guilt.

So my advice to you is to get your life in order. Work on the most important things first; then you can work on your golf swing and your suntan. Don't pour your life into anything or anyone who cannot pour something back into one or more of these important areas of your life. Devote your time and energy primarily to those people who lie at the center of your world, and do those things in life that can give you the greatest return on your investment.

I'm not just talking about money here; I'm talking about the investments that lead to satisfaction and significance. If there is something in your heart that consumes you and it is noble and it just won't go away, that dream is probably what you need to be doing with your life. And if you have failed at that goal in the past, but it still won't go away, then you definitely need to try it again. But you don't need to let it consume you to the point that you lose your sense of balance in life.

If you want to be a medical professional, for instance, and you are thinking about returning to school even though you had to drop out the first time around, go ahead and take another shot at your dream. And when you do take that shot, give it your all. Make sure you have cleared your schedule of all unnecessary distractions so you can focus the next few years on pursuing your education and building the relationships and the practical experience you will need to succeed as a medical professional.

At the same time, however, don't harm yourself by damaging those parts of your life that will endure long after this chapter of your life has ended. Don't sacrifice your spiritual life for an office and a title. Don't neglect your family, your true friends, and the people who have poured themselves into you over the course of your life just so you can raise your grade point average a tenth of a point. Keep your life balanced. The "ball" of your education may be at the apex of your circle during this particular season in life, but you still need to avoid dropping the other important balls because, in time, those other balls will work their way back to the top of your focus and your educational pursuits will drop to the bottom. And never forget that the professional part of your life is incomplete unless you have someone to share it with and someone whose life you can enrich with the prosperity your success has generated.

So let passion drive you toward the things you want to achieve, but don't let your passion blind you to the other facets of your life that are just as important. Don't let your dreams become "idols" in your life. Place them high on your list of priorities, but make sure you keep them in context. Every aspect of your life will find its meaning in the context of every other thing you do.

A BALANCE OF SACRIFICE

Another word for "sacrifice" is "investment." Think about it! Every time you make an investment, you sacrifice something today in the hope of multiplying it in the future. To make a financial investment in the stock market, for instance, you must sacrifice the hard-earned money you would like to spend today in the hope that your investment will produce more money for you tomorrow. Right now, therefore, you don't get to enjoy the benefits that your money could provide, but you do get to look forward to greater benefits tomorrow.

Likewise, to make an investment of your time in building your own business is to forego spending your time doing the things you would prefer to do instead. Your long-range goal of course is to build something that can provide income for you so you won't have to work so hard in your senior years. But for now, that's just a dream. For now, you are working a full-time job and putting every spare minute of your personal time into building something that isn't producing anything for you at the moment. You are making an investment. You are making a sacrifice with the hope of earning a future return.

For this reason, consider carefully the investment you are willing to make in your dream. On the one hand, don't make the mistake of investing too little. A great dream cannot be birthed with a half-hearted commitment or an insufficient down payment. Great dreams require great faith, and great faith requires great sacrifice. So understand upfront that a real dream requires a substantial monetary investment before it yields any results, and a real dream requires a significant investment of one's time. Avoid the trap of self-deception. No notable achievement is easy, and nothing is as simple as it appears. You will have to pay in advance for the success you want in the future.

On the other hand, it is possible to pour too much into a dream. You can be too hasty, too extreme, and too impatient. Like the man who puts his last dime on his lucky number at the roulette wheel, you can be foolish. And you can easily neglect your health, your marriage, your children, and your own soul if you don't give reasonable attention to the more enduring things in your life.

So keep things in balance. If you truly believe in the worthiness of your dream and your ability to achieve it, you will give your dream every chance for success by giving it every dollar you can squeeze out of your budget and every available minute you can squeeze out of your life. But no sane individual takes the rent money to buy risky stocks. And no responsible human being takes the shoes off his children's feet to mass-market the hydro-capacitor widget he invented in the shed behind his house. A sane and responsible person sacrifices what he can. He makes intentional plans to temporarily cut back on other expenditures and other pursuits in order to have more time and money during a specific season of his life when he is putting greater emphasis on the pursuit of his goals. But he refuses to neglect the other important parts of his life or to neglect them to his own detriment. No matter how focused he might be on his dream, he never drops his other balls.

A BALANCE OF EXPECTATIONS

I like passionate people. Only passionate people succeed in the long run, and only passionate people can make the sacrifices that are necessary for success in great endeavors. But passion is just one inch shy of insanity, and insanity can be destructive. So balance is necessary if a passionate person intends to avoid falling over the cliff.

A passionate person makes his dreams a high priority in his life, but a balanced person makes sure that he is successfully juggling all the important parts of his life. A passionate person sacrifices to make his dreams come true. He invests in his dreams and sacrifices certain things today with the full expectation of enlarging his life in the future. But a balanced person doesn't invest anything more than he has available. He doesn't borrow irresponsibly or steal from others what he lacks while pursuing his goals.

If you have fallen short in the past, therefore, I encourage you to try again and to give your dream everything you have. But that's it. You cannot give more than you possess. You have to keep things in balance because, if you don't, you will fail in other important areas of your life. A person who is balanced will not only allocate his time and his resources wisely while keeping his priorities in healthy alignment; he also will have reasonable expectations for his life. And he will be able to separate "today" and "tomorrow" in his own mind.

A person with a vision for his life tends to focus on tomorrow more than today, and that is understandable. After all, the realization of a vision lies in the future and requires a reasonable sacrifice of today's time and treasures. But a person of balance knows how to pursue tomorrow without squandering today. He knows how to make the necessary sacrifices today that can result in the desired ends tomorrow, but he knows how to make those sacrifices without losing the good things he holds in his hand right now.

There are things in your life today that you won't have

tomorrow, so you would be foolish to waste the blessings you actually have in order to chase a dream that may not turn out the way you imagined. Only a fool, for instance, would throw away the experience of his children's growing years to pursue a vain imagination. And only a fool would ignore the wife of his youth to chase a fantasy that is unachievable. Tomorrow will certainly be empty and meaningless if you don't invest something into making it what you want it to be, and the more you invest, the greater the return will be. But today can be just as empty if you focus so strongly on tomorrow that you fail to appreciate the value of the things you have right now.

As you know, I love dreamers, and I love people who are passionate about the things they want to do. Visionaries are those who make life worth living. They are the people who make things happen in our world. But if visionaries have an Achilles' heel, it's that they are so consumed by tomorrow they cannot enjoy today, even when today is filled with joy and wonders and the fulfillment of many past dreams.

So don't fall into this trap. Don't be so heavenly minded that you are no earthly good, and don't be so future oriented that you are worthless to yourself and others right now. Instead, enjoy today while pursuing tomorrow. Laugh today while working toward tomorrow. Live a full life today while planning for tomorrow and working for tomorrow. In other words, be balanced. Do everything you do with one foot in the present and the other foot in the future. Don't go to extremes, and realize that patience is the virtue you need the most.

There is great wisdom in this approach to life, a wisdom that many people, including me, have gained from our past failures and second shots. You simply cannot succeed without passion, but you can certainly fail if you don't learn to harness your passion and make it work for you. You cannot succeed without determination, but you can certainly make a determined mess of things if you don't learn how to control your energy and channel it so it doesn't create imbalance in your life. Remember, nuclear energy is a powerful and constructive force, providing people around the world with a higher quality of life than they would be able to enjoy without it. But if it is used without prudence and caution, nuclear energy can kill millions of people. And so can passion that is not channeled within the context of a well-balanced life.

Zig Ziglar, one of America's most renowned writers, said, "I believe that being successful means having a balance of success stories across the many areas of your life. You can't truly be considered successful in your business life if your home life is in shambles." And Brian Tracy, another well-known speaker and writer, said, "Just as your car runs more smoothly and requires less energy to go faster and farther when the wheels are in perfect alignment, you perform better when your thoughts, feelings, emotions, goals, and values are in balance."

As it is in golf, in basketball, and in juggling, so it is in life: It's about maintaining your balance. Balance is the essential ingredient for a winning game and for a fulfilling life. It is the essential element that you need to be successful in both the present and the future. So I encourage you to consider what is truly important to you and to determine that you will be a passionate player in the game of life, relishing all the joys of today while preparing for the rewards of tomorrow and keeping your many colorful balls in the air without dropping any of them.

CONTACT

Never mistake activity for achievement.
—John Wooden

E VERY SPORT involves intense competition, and many sports involve direct contact with other players. Basketball is one of those "contact" sports. In fact, there is simply no way to play the game of basketball without making contact with the other players on the court. Unlike football, where contact is an intentional part of the game, basketball is not designed for intentional contact. Contact in basketball is simply a byproduct of movement rather than a deliberate act. Nevertheless, when you have ten players running, blocking, scrambling for loose balls, and jumping in a confined space to shoot at the goal or retrieve loose balls, contact is inevitable.

Many people who are unfamiliar with the game of basketball mistakenly believe that basketball is a non-physical sport. But basketball players put their hands on one another all the time in an effort to keep up with the players they are defending, and rebounders beneath the basket push and shove one another constantly in an effort to establish position for rebounding missed shots.

So basketball truly is a rough sport. And sportswriters are beginning to really talk about the physical nature of the evolving game. For instance, in the *Times-News* of Elon, North Carolina, a January 26, 2013, article about the local Elon University basketball team said, "It would not surprise me if the Elon University men's basketball team members receive varsity letters in wrestling at the end of the season."

The article, written by Don Bolden, describes the physical nature of play at this proud institution. "They seem to be spending a lot of time on the floor this year," Bolden notes, "as the sport seems to become rougher with each passing season.... And because of all this, it is not unusual to see players with huge braces on a knee, on an ankle, all the way up an entire leg, and on shoulders and elbows. Nor is it unusual to see a player on the bench in street clothes waiting for a serious injury to heal before returning to the game. It's a rough game."

But in the same way that basketball is a rough game, life is a rough game too. And in the same way that basketball provides a lot of contact that leads to a lot of injuries, life provides a lot of contact that leads to a lot of injuries. Before you decide to reenter the game, therefore, you need to come to grips with this reality.

STOP BEFORE IT'S TOO LATE

Life is a contact sport. There's a lot of pushing and shoving in the game of life, and there's a lot of wounds that result from the conflict. You cannot move through life with your eyes on a goal and avoid making some serious contact with others in a way that can leave you bruised and hurting. You are going to constantly interact with other people on your drive to the goal, so you need to learn quickly how to take the punishment and how to make contact in a "clean" way without committing a "foul."

Contact in basketball can quickly escalate into conflict if the players aren't careful, and trouble is often conceived in those moments of conflict when otherwise sane human beings lose control. In fact, all of us have seen these episodes in athletic competition. In highly competitive basketball games, for instance, the players sometimes clear the benches and run onto the court for an old-fashioned, all-out brawl. In football, too, blows are sometimes thrown and players occasionally spark broader scuffles because they lose control of their emotions in the heat of combat. And in hockey and baseball, the problem is even more common. But there are ways that the officials can deal with these inappropriate displays of anger.

The consequence of excessive contact in hockey is the penalty box. In baseball, it's ejection. And in basketball, the penalty for committing a flagrant-2 foul (contact that is deliberate and which exceeds the boundaries of sportsmanlike conduct) is ejection and possible fines and suspension. In life, too, reasonable contact is to be expected among people competing for the limited rewards of life. But unreasonable or deliberate contact is intolerable, and it creates situations where lasting damage can be done both to the victims and the perpetrators of the action. And that's when extra wisdom is required to handle the conflicts that flow from excessive contact so that unpleasant consequences won't occur.

A friend of mine played football at a high school in Georgia that was well known at the time for its championship teams. The coach there was a local legend, and he led his players to several national rankings at the high school level. But the coach was just as concerned about building young men of character as he was in developing his players as athletes, and he often lectured his players on life and how to handle conflict on and off the field. The quote that my friend remembers most fondly is the occasion when his coach told the team, "Men, football is not a contact sport. Kissing is a contact sport. Football is a collision sport." And how true that is.

But sometimes in life, we find ourselves moving past the point of simple contact and even the point of conflict as we work our way into a collision course with certain people around us. Because of this tendency, therefore, I believe it is critical to have a plan in place for those times of possible "collision" when disaster looms on the horizon, the predictable times of excessive conflict when you do not agree with the other person, when you are in discord, or even when you are in the throes of outright controversy.

I have a checklist that I run through in my own mind when circumstances like this begin to emerge in my life, and this mental checklist has helped me many times to slow down and make a wise choice rather than rushing headlong into a situation where my initial words or actions can be damaging. I use the acrostic "SLOW" to help me deal with conflict resolution, and the word itself is a reminder that to rush is often to stumble.

S = STOP. Stop right where you are. If you are in a situation that is creating immediate tension, remove yourself without hesitation. Don't say anything; don't do anything. Just stop. You need a few minutes, or perhaps longer, to make sure you have a handle on yourself and your own emotions before proceeding. So get away from the source of the trouble. Go to another room, walk outside, or, if none of these options are available, just shut down and refuse to say anything. Take as much time as you need to compose yourself, because it is essential that you maintain control of your thoughts, actions, and reactions before you respond to a tense situation. Remember, you are not responsible for the words and actions of other people, but you are responsible for yourself. So don't let anyone goad you into precipitous action. Stop and regroup.

L = LISTEN. Quite often, conflict arises because of miscommunication. So don't let that happen. Go back to the person with whom you are disagreeing and start the conversation over. But this time, don't interrupt, don't interpret, and don't infer.

Just listen and hear the other person out. Sometimes people just want to vent. If this resolves the conflict, great! If this fails to solve the problem, then at least you will know the other person's position and you will have lowered the heat by giving that person an opportunity to express himself. So listen carefully and listen intentionally.

O = OPTIONS. The most important skill in conflict resolution is the ability to negotiate. The ability to reach a compromise through options that are acceptable to both sides is the most important skill a person can possibly possess when it comes to turning a relational problem into a winning situation. So if you can work with the other party to create a plan where both of you feel you are better off, both of you will win. Be open, therefore, to some options other than "your way or the highway," because your way may not be the right way in the end and it certainly is not the only way to solve your dilemma. If you plan to succeed in life where you have failed in the past, you must learn to treat the other person with the same respect that you want to receive from him, and you must learn to see the world through that person's eyes, not just your own. So come up with a plan. Come up with more than just one solution to your problem. And learn to be creative with your options.

W = WORK. A simple disagreement can end just as quickly as it started. But sometimes, conflict doesn't stem from a simple disagreement. Sometimes, conflict is the result of something that has been brewing for a long time. If this is the case, the problem you are confronting won't be resolved in one conversation. You will have to be committed to working on the problem. You also must be willing to work on your attitude. If not, you can expect the same unpleasant situation to repeat itself, and each incident of conflict can easily exceed the previous episodes in duration and intensity. It takes work and a concerted effort to rebuild a wounded relationship. So prepare yourself to do some hard work, knowing that the end result will be worth the effort.

Conflict is inevitable in life, but resolution is always possible when we are willing to do things the right way. So when one of your relationships hits a snag and is threatened by unnecessary discord, SLOW down in order to keep a temporary problem from becoming a permanent one. By having a plan in place to deal with conflict in your relationships, you will be much less susceptible to disaster when one of those relationships hits some unexpected turbulence.

But rather than dealing with conflict in a proactive way, some people tend to just give up when they are confronted with opposition. They become disappointed and overwhelmed when they finally realize that life is not always the easy road they thought it was going to be. All of us grow up with childhood expectations of life. And usually, these expectations flow not from reality, but from fantasies or from a distorted view of reality that was bequeathed to us by others when we were too young to know the difference. But sometimes we never grow out of these fantasies and illusions, and we fail to come to grips with our unrealistic expectations of life. So if you haven't caught on yet, know right now that not every event in your life will end "happily ever after" and not every damsel in distress will be rescued by a handsome prince. Life is wonderful; there's no doubt about it. But life isn't always filled with fairy godmothers and talking horses.

WELCOME TO THE REAL WORLD

I have always said that discouragement is the natural consequence of unrealistic expectations, because, when you have an expectation in any area of your life that is not rooted in reality, you are setting yourself up for disappointment and failure. You are setting yourself up to lose. And this might have something to do with your previous failed attempts in life. Perhaps you expected things from the government, from yourself, or from other people that you had no right to expect, and you became disillusioned because of your unfounded hopes. Or perhaps you couldn't handle the conflict and the contact that resulted from your efforts to do a good thing in the right way. Perhaps you thought life was supposed to be a wonderful game where everybody laughed and played together while encouraging one another and helping one another. And because of these false assumptions, you have now become sour, cynical, and perhaps a little bitter. You learned the hard way and the painful way that life is filled with a lot of competition and not everybody has your best interests in mind. And now you are living with the scars of these hard lessons.

Don't get me wrong: I believe in dreams. I believe in having a vision for my life. But the truth is that life is tough and life is unfair. Life also is problematic and competitive. And that is not a bad thing. That is not evil. In fact, it's the way things ought to be because honest competition makes us better and honest conflict makes things better for those we serve. Conflict makes us better because it sharpens us and makes our failures more painful so we won't be inclined to repeat them. And competition makes things better because it forces us to provide better products and better services at a faster pace and a lower price. So pure competition is good, and conflict is the natural consequence of competition. With no opposition and no challenges, life would be dull indeed and life would be unexceptional.

Have you ever seen that episode of the *Twilight Zone* where the gambling man dies and appears to go to the great casino in the sky? There, in "heaven," he starts to play, and he starts to win. And he continues to win … and win … and win. In fact, every time he plays, he wins. So he has everything he wants. He has only to wish it, and it happens.

At first, this is great. The guy is really enjoying himself. In time, however, the euphoria turns into frustration, and the frustration turns into misery. And soon, the man realizes that his greatest joy in life was not winning; his greatest joy was the work, the effort, the challenge, and the risk associated with pursuing what is rare and difficult to attain. So satisfaction is not found in beating the game. Satisfaction is found in playing the game, in competing, and in knowing that what you are doing is indeed unusual. If the outcome is guaranteed in advance, your actions and your efforts suddenly become meaningless.

So do not wish for an easy life. You will never grow if you stay in your comfort zone. Instead, embrace the conflict and the contact. Know that through the struggle comes the satisfaction of winning and of meeting opposition and emerging victorious. In the game of life that you and I play every day, you either prevail in the competitive world or you lose ground in the competitive world. That's just the way it is.

THE POSITIVE EFFECTS OF CONFLICT

William Ellery Channing, an impassioned preacher from the early nineteenth century, said, "Difficulties are meant to rouse, not discourage. The human spirit is to grow strong by conflict." Conflict and competition, therefore, are good things, not bad things. They are like forest fires. Although they leave temporary scars on the landscape, they produce long-term health for the forest. And that is why struggle is woven into the fabric of life. It is there to make us stronger, to make us better, and to make us humbler as we ascend the summit of success. Struggle should never be allowed to cripple us.

Conflict and competition sharpen us, they refine us, and they keep us on our toes even after we have become the best at what we do. So even though these particular elements of life may be uncomfortable at times and less pleasant than the more enjoyable aspects of our pursuits, they are necessary for greatness, and they are essential for excellence. The "tension" that contact creates in our lives keeps everything in balance and keeps everything simple, fresh, and focused.

One of the greatest tragedies in sports and in life is that too many participants seek success without considering the price of success, they seek fame without realizing what makes a person truly famous, and they seek happiness without understanding the foundations of true happiness. A rising star in basketball knows that he wants to be a renowned player, and he knows that he wants to be celebrated during his career and beyond. But success in basketball, as in life, comes only to those who have faced the competition, prevailing in those battles. And happiness comes to those who have endured great conflicts and have stood to tell the tale.

But I believe the wrong concept of happiness often leads people down the wrong path in life. It seems that many times a person starts out with great goals and worthy ideals. But as his life unfolds, these noble dreams are often exchanged for childish wishes regarding a specific job or a specific person or a certain salary or a house in a particular neighborhood. And the person begins to put his hopes and dreams and even his own identity into those things that can never give him a true return on his emotional investment.

In fact, we see this pattern all the time. Celebrities constantly tell us that their fame and fortune have failed to bring them the happiness they thought it would. Parents spend enormous amounts of time and money trying to make their little children content. And virtually every day we hear a coworker say, "I'm quitting; I'm just not happy." So apparently, we are consumed with achieving a real sense of happiness. Unfortunately, in spite of our ceaseless efforts, most of us never seem to grasp this elusive prize.

Perhaps that is why novelist William S. Burroughs wrote, "Happiness is a byproduct of function, purpose, and conflict; those who seek happiness for itself seek victory without war." Happiness, therefore, is not a worthy goal, and neither is success. We cannot hope to achieve happiness by chasing after happiness or achieve success by striving for success, because happiness and success can never be earned or apprehended. Rather, they are byproducts of worthy quests. They are the consequence of doing noble things. And Burroughs makes it clear that they are obtained by pursuing worthy ideals and prevailing against daunting foes.

So my advice to you as you prepare to reengage the goals that once captivated your heart is to stop chasing the end products of your dream and start giving yourself to the present activities that will make your dream a reality. Stop longing for the end result, and simply walk the path that will take you there. Satisfaction is found in the pursuit, and happiness is found in the journey rather than the arrival. But conflict is an inevitable part of that journey; it is a necessary element on the pathway to achievement.

Consequently, there is no dishonor in competition, and there is no evil in conflict. Evil is present or absent in our lives when we decide the manner in which we will conduct ourselves in competition and the way we will handle the presence of conflict. But the conflict itself is not evil, and the competition is not unjust. In fact, nature itself teaches us that conflict and competition are good things and necessary things. They are the natural consequence of two people with noble intentions crossing paths while pursuing their respective goals. They are the natural consequence of two entities vying for the same prize. So there is nothing intentional about such a struggle, and there is nothing unseemly about it either. And for this reason, we should learn to accept the reality of competition and to handle conflict with pure hearts.

THE NECESSARY COMBAT OF LIFE

About 2,400 years ago, Plato wrote, "I exhort you also to take part in the great combat, which is the combat of life, and greater than every other earthly conflict." Plato thought it advantageous to encourage men to embrace conflict rather than avoid it because he understood the essence of life and the essence of success. He also understood that nothing is worth having unless it is worth the battle you must fight to attain it. And he knew that when many people compete for a single award or the singular achievement of being the best at what they do, conflict is inevitable and the competition is endless. But whenever something worthwhile is accomplished by overcoming one's own limitations or by rising above the impediments to success that are often raised by doubters, obstructionists, and competitors, the reward for that achievement is sweeter, and the satisfaction is more enduring.

This is why nobody understands competition and conflict better than an athlete. But for a basketball player, the battle is not personal; it is the nature of the game. First, he must compete with himself. He must overcome his own appetites and his own bad habits in order to demonstrate resolve in the mastery of his sport. Then he must resist those who would hinder him by interfering with his pursuits or by criticizing his efforts. He must also oppose those who are vying for the position in the lineup that he is seeking for himself, and he must skillfully battle the other members of his own team so he can earn a starting position. Finally, on the court, he must engage the opposing players. He must tirelessly outwit the player who is trying to keep him from scoring, and he must work hard to score against the player who is guarding him, all while fighting fatigue, fighting discouragement, and contending with the referees and the crowd.

But in the same way that a basketball player can compete without internalizing the conflict and can fight hard against his opponent without demonstrating poor sportsmanship, you too can fight hard to do your best and to be your best without slipping over the line into illegal activity or immoral behavior. You can outperform others without slandering them. You can do a better job and produce a better product without showing contempt for those who compete in your arena. You can be your best without crossing legal lines.

There is nothing wrong with competition, but there is everything wrong with animosity. There is nothing wrong with conflict, but there is everything wrong with hurting other people or damaging their reputations. A good basketball player knows how to dig in and establish position without injuring his opponent, and a good basketball player knows how to push back beneath the basket without committing a foul. You, too, need to learn that competition is the name of the game and that conflict is a way of life. Don't let the fear of these things keep you from taking another shot at your goals. But at the same time, don't let these things change you into a person you don't want to be. Accept the competitive nature of life, and be willing to take some lumps as you fight for your place on the team. But don't ever let the game change you inside. Do everything right and with a noble heart. Fight the good fight.

TIMING

Seize the moment, and the hour will be yours.
—Anonymous

TEN YEARS after the 9/11 terrorist attacks on the United States, CNN ran a story about several individuals who should have been in the World Trade Center or on one of the fated airline flights that horrific day. But for unforeseen reasons, the routine schedules of these people were inexplicably changed in a way that saved their lives.

One man stopped by the post office on the way to his brokerage job at a firm located on the 96th floor of the North Tower. He then attempted to board the express train to downtown, but it was overcrowded. So being claustrophobic, he decided to take the local train instead, even though it was slower. This caused the man to be late for work, and that unexpected delay ended up saving his life. As he was approaching the building entrance, the first plane struck the tower, killing 295 people in his office. Timing!

A few days earlier, a United Airlines flight attendant entered the wrong code into the computer system while setting up her work schedule for September and was not awarded her normal flights from Boston to California for that month. In an effort to rectify the mistake, however, the flight attendant managed to trade all her flights back to her normal schedule except for the flight on 9/11. She still had an assignment to fly to Denver that day instead of Los Angeles. Then on September 10th, while she was trying to make this final change back to her original schedule, the computer system froze, causing her to miss the deadline by just one minute. So the next morning, her flight to Denver left Logan International Airport, leaving the runway between American Flight 11 (her usual flight, which struck the North Tower) and United Flight 175, the flight that crashed into the South Tower that same morning. Timing!

TIMING IS EVERYTHING

Everything in life is a matter of timing, whether we recognize it or not. Your greatest successes have occurred as a result of opportunity meeting need at just the right moments in time, and your greatest failures have occurred as a result of difficulty meeting resistance at precisely the worst moments in time. I cannot explain why life happens this way, but we all know that it does.

So life is about timing. If you have ever tried to teach a child how to hit a baseball, you know both the frustration of poor timing and the exhilaration of good timing. And those same feelings of frustration and exhilaration can carry over into the more important aspects of our lives as well, because most of what we accomplish depends on the proper timing of the uncontrollable events affecting us.

That's why, when someone has a good sense of timing, what we are really saying is that the person has the ability to select the precise moment for doing something to achieve the optimum result. And all of us know from our own personal experiences just how important this sense of selection can be. Timing is what makes the difference between a good joke and a bad one. Timing is what makes the difference between success and failure in a job search. Timing is what makes the difference between closing the sale and losing it. Timing is even important in the practice of medicine, because some people live and some people die solely on the basis of the timing of a diagnosis or treatment.

So those in pursuit of success are usually focused on the timing of their deeds. They know that the actions they take to achieve their goals can easily have different outcomes depending on the timing of those actions. And I am reminded of this reality every time I think about the sister of one of my good friends, who died when she was a child from heart complications resulting from strep throat. Because my friend's sister was born in the 1930s, the proper medicine was not available at that time. But if the same thing should happen to a child today, antibiotics would be used and the child would have a high likelihood of surviving with no lingering effects. Timing impacts every aspect of our lives.

Timing impacts sports too, In fact, if there is one thing that every sport has in common, it's timing. Especially in a game like basketball, which is governed by multiple "clocks," timing is an essential element of the game. In basketball, the game clock determines when play begins and ends. The shot clock displays the time remaining before a team must shoot the ball. And the officials are always keeping other "clocks" in their heads, because players are not allowed to stand in certain areas indefinitely or to hold the ball without consideration for the passing seconds. The game must move forward with deliberation. In this sport, time is of the essence.

Timing in basketball is important in another regard, too, because the difference between a slam dunk and a blocked shot can be hundredths of a second. And the difference between a game-winning three-pointer and a game-losing air ball can be milliseconds, as well. In fact, victory in track and field events and in swimming contests in the Olympic Games is literally measured in thousandths of a second, and some of the greatest athletic performances of all time have come within the blink of an eye of failing.

In 2008, for instance, in Beijing, China, American swimmer Michael Phelps defeated Serbia's Milorad Cavic by just .01 seconds to clinch the gold medal in the 100-meter butterfly. In 1988, Anthony Nesty of the little island nation of Suriname defeated American swimmer Matt Biondi by the same margin for the gold medal in the same event. And in the 1972 Summer Olympic Games in Munich, Germany, American Tim McKee lost a gold medal in the 400-meter individual medley by a mere two one-thousandths (.002) of a second.

But timing in sports isn't about just beating the clock; timing also involves beating the opposition. How many slow-motion replays of a great three-point shot have you seen that showed the ball clearing the defender's outstretched arm by a fraction of an inch? Or how many long-distance kicks in soccer have you seen soar past the goalie's long arms by a matter of inches only to find the top right-hand corner of the net by a couple of centimeters?

Timing is everything. In baseball, the difference between a highlight-reel home run and a hard-swinging strikeout can be a matter of a fraction of a second in the timing of the batter's swing. In football, the difference between a receiver catching the downfield bomb and dropping it off the ends of his fingers can be a matter of a half of a fraction of a second. In hockey, the difference between the game-winning goal and another rejected shot can be the blink of an eye. And a player can't spike a volley-ball unless his jump is timed perfectly. So athletic competition depends on timing as much as it depends on talent, skill, and determination. On the professional level, athletes are forced to even time their pre-game meals in order to maximize their performance during the game.

Timing is important in investing, too. The difference between a rich man and a poor man is often the timing of that person's purchases and the timing of his sell-offs. The man who buys real estate cheap and sells it when the market is red-hot can get rich really quick. But the man who invests in real estate, stocks, or precious metals when the price is high can easily lose his shirt. Just imagine, for instance, what your portfolio would look like today if you had bought gold in 1999 when it was $252.80 an ounce or if you had bought stock in Google when it was available for $85 per share.

And timing is important in relationships. When you met your spouse, you met that person at an opportune time. If you had met your mate when he or she was involved in another relationship, you might well have missed the opportunity to know that person and certainly would have missed the opportunity to nurture a romance. Quite often, everyday guys catch the most amazing girls simply because they crossed paths with her at just the right time in her life.

THE IMPORTANCE OF TIMING

If you really think about it, everything in your life happened as a result of timing. You met your best friend because the two of you were in the same place at the same time, doing the same thing during a parallel season in your lives. You bought your house because it was available for sale at the precise moment you were ready to buy. You found your current job because your company was looking to hire on the same day you were looking for employment. And you first became fascinated in your favorite hobby when someone instrumental in your life introduced you to that activity at a time when you were open to something new.

The smart people among us have learned the value of time and the necessity of timing their big leaps into the vast unknown. In fact, American humorist Arnold Glasow has famously said, "Success is simple. Do what's right, the right way, at the right time." And that pretty much sums it up.

Look at Mark Zuckerberg, for instance. Zuckerberg became a billionaire at the ripe old age of 23 as a result of his pioneering work with Facebook, and he is currently estimated to be worth almost $34 billion (*Forbes* 400 richest Americans) even though he is just 30 years old. But Zuckerberg's success can be attributed in large part to his innate sense of timing.

Just think about it! Facebook was not the first social media networking site, just as Google was not the first search engine or YouTube the first video-sharing site. At least five other companies beat Facebook to the punch. But Zuckerberg knew the value of timing. He rolled out his product incrementally and then went for it full throttle when he thought the timing was right in the marketplace. And the results have been astounding.

I know that my own success on many occasions has been the result of divine timing. Several times in my life, I have been in just the right place at just the right time so I could make my talents available to someone who needed them at that moment, and those providential alignments of events have catapulted me into numerous unforeseen opportunities in my professional and personal life. You, too, need to consider the significance of timing as you contemplate a renewed shot at your dreams.

Every dream—whether it involves the pursuit of wealth, success, romance, or any other worthy goal—will succeed or fail depending upon the timing of the effort. In this regard, life is a lot like the weather. There are dozens of factors affecting the atmospheric conditions of a particular spot on the globe. There's temperature, humidity, wind direction, wind velocity, ocean currents, barometric pressure, and even pollen content, just to name a few. But a perfect day is the result of the alignment of all these variables in a particular way. And a perfect storm is the result of the same thing.

Not long ago, I read an article about the sinking of the *Titanic*. The author had conducted extensive research on the people listed on the ship's manifest, including those passengers who sailed on the *Titanic* and the ones who bought a ticket and never showed up. Among those left behind was Henry Clay Frick, the Pittsburgh steel baron, and his wife, Adelaide. The couple had booked tickets to return to New York on the maiden voyage of the *Titanic,* but Adelaide sprained her ankle in Italy and had to be hospitalized. And because of this unpredictable event, Henry and Adelaide missed "the disaster of the century."

Another booked passenger, Milton Hershey, founder of The Hershey Chocolate Company, and his wife, Kitty, had spent the winter in France and had purchased tickets to return to the United States on the *Titanic*. However, at the last minute, the "chocolate king" took an earlier departure on the *SS Amerika* because of pressing business matters back home.

So the timing of almost everything—particularly the execution of our plans—has a profound impact on our lives. It has a profound impact on the quality of our lives, too, and it has a profound impact on the outcome of our lives.

TIMING CONTROL

From 1998 to 2001, United Paramount Network (UPN) produced a television show entitled *Seven Days*. The storyline for the 66 episodes of this short-lived series was that a secret branch of the NSA had developed a "Chronosphere" that provided one person with the ability to travel back in time for seven days (thus the title of the show). According to the NSA rules, however, time travel was only to be used to avert disasters related to national security. Nevertheless, this amazing machine afforded this particular government agency the opportunity to send someone back in time to "correct" things that had gone awry during the preceding week.

The interesting thing to me about the show was the attitude that this ability spawned among the few people who knew about the Chronosphere's existence and who took turns participating in time travel. The people who were part of this project no longer saw events as permanent or their actions as consequential. Instead, they became careless in their decision-making because they knew that, if any national security action they might take should deteriorate into a dangerous situation, they could always fix the problem with a do-over.

Unfortunately, we don't have that luxury. I have a washing machine in my house and you probably have one too, but neither of us have a Chronosphere. So even though we would love to be able to press a redo button whenever things go wrong in our lives, we can't. It sure would be nice sometimes if we could simply go back a week and erase the mistakes we have made. But we don't have that luxury. Instead, our actions are permanent. Once we say that word or do that deed, once we act or react, we must move on and deal with the consequences of our choices, whether good or bad, profitable or unprofitable. But even though we can't usually undo the things we have done, we can always take another shot at things and try to do them better.

In consideration of this truth, therefore, my advice to you is to do everything you can do to control the timing of your next shot. Give yourself the best chance for success by choosing the time you will take action and the time you will put your resources at risk. When it is time to be aggressive, for instance, move forward with determination, and you will outpace those who oppose you. When it is time to be fearless, press the accelerator, and you will magnify your opportunities to "win" while minimizing your opportunities to "lose." When it is time to be strong, take your stand and position yourself for the rebound that is destined to come your way, and take the follow-up shot you need to take once you have regained possession of the ball. The traits God has placed within you and the qualities you have honed over the course of your life are there to equip you for victory, but none of your strengths can guarantee you success if you utilize them with poor timing, and none of your resources can give you an advantage in the game of life if you expend them without consideration of the conditions you confront. In the end, you cannot fly a kite on a windless day.

Maybe bad timing had something to do with your previous failures, maybe it didn't. But regardless of what may have gone wrong in your past attempts, as you seek to control the timing of your next shot, be aware of the contributing factors that will play a role in the success or failure of your venture. What is it that you want to accomplish? Does in involve business? If so, you will need to carefully time your entry into the marketplace. A product offered at the wrong time to the wrong people at the wrong price won't stand a chance in the free market. Does it involve an idea? If so, you will need to carefully time the presentation of your concept. Scott Adams, the creator of the *Dilbert* comic strip, once said, "Your best work involves timing. If someone wrote the greatest hip-hop song of all time during the Middle Ages, he had bad timing."

The highway of history is littered with the corpses of forgotten people who had great ideas ahead of their time or who failed to offer their ideas when the culture was poised to embrace them. But virtually every great achievement that has ever been recorded was an achievement accomplished by someone who took an existing idea and reintroduced it to the world in just the right way at just the right time.

If you would take a moment to review your life, you would probably find that the difference between your biggest successes and your biggest failures—between your proudest achievements and your poorest ones—has not been the quality of your ideas or the motives behind them. The difference has probably been timing. Most of your failures probably flowed from good intentions and noble ambitions, and most of your disappointments probably grew out of sincere and wholehearted efforts. But failed businesses, failed relationships, and failed political careers are more often the result of poor timing than poor planning, poor ideas, or poor execution.

ADJUST YOUR TIMING

Because of these things, give some careful and attentive thought to the timing of your next shot. Don't just throw the ball back up at the goal as if the clock were expiring. Run your offense, plan your attack, set yourself, and pick the spot from which you want to shoot. Don't try to force the action. In basketball and in life, let the opportunity come to you; don't try to make things happen that aren't happening naturally.

This doesn't mean that you should wait forever, because eventually the shot clock will expire. And this doesn't mean that you should approach your goals in a passive way either, because windows of opportunity don't stay open forever. But the need for proper timing requires that you take reasonable precautions to make sure you are not forcing things to happen when it's not the right time or the right environment for them to happen.

Hesiod, the Greek poet who lived around 700 BC, said, "Observe due measure, for right timing is in all things the most important factor." And Miyamoto Musashi, a notoriously gifted

Japanese swordsman from the early seventeenth century, said, "You win battles by knowing the enemy's timing and using a timing which the enemy does not expect."

The Bible also is replete with advice regarding the importance of timing, because the writers of Scripture understood the value of good timing in life. King Solomon, for instance, paints a picture in the book of Ecclesiastes of how timing can positively or negatively affect the outcome of everyday events. Solomon writes: "There is a time for everything, and a season for every activity under the heavens: a time to be born and a time to die, a time to plant and a time to uproot, a time to kill and a time to heal, a time to tear down and a time to build, a time to weep and a time to laugh, a time to mourn and a time to dance, a time to scatter stones and a time to gather them, a time to embrace and a time to refrain from embracing, a time to search and a time to give up, a time to keep and a time to throw away, a time to tear and a time to mend, a time to be silent and a time to speak, a time to love and a time to hate, a time for war and a time for peace" (Ecclesiastes 3:1-8, NIV).

So here's the thing: If you have failed in the past, you need to understand *why* you failed before you try taking another shot. If you can find the reasons behind your previous failures, you will dramatically increase your chances for future success, because you will be wiser and better equipped with the knowledge you need to do things right this time around. You will be more inclined to avoid the pitfalls that resulted in your demise earlier in your life, and you will probably make better decisions that will lead to smarter planning and more fruitful tactics. Success is never guaranteed, but the chances of success are always increased when we learn something from past failures. That is why so many successful people have past histories of foolish blunders.

But if you don't have a good grasp on why you failed the first time, you are probably destined to fail again, at least partially. And there's a good chance that poor timing was a factor in your downfall. If you tried to build a business on borrowed money when interest rates were at record highs or if you tried to manufacture pagers when cell phones were the newest rage, then you had poor timing. If you tried to capitalize on the disco craze when discos were on their way out or if you invested all your money in horsewhips just as Henry Ford was setting up shop in Detroit, then you had poor timing.

So this time, use some common sense: Don't ignore the signs on the horizon. Understand the times in which you live and the mindset of the masses as you prepare to engage them. Be contemporary. Be relevant. Sense the direction the wind is blowing and set your sails to take advantage of those wind currents, not to paddle upstream against it. And if you aren't completely confident in your assessment of future trends, seek the input of others who have their ears to the ground. Read books. Attend seminars. Ask questions. Network with people who seem to have a grip on market movements, and pay attention to forecasts regarding future trends in society. When you take your next shot, you will either need a game plan that will always be relevant (people will always need to buy food, for instance) or you will need a game plan that is flexible and can bend with the blowing winds of change (technology changes almost daily). So make your plans, and plan your timing.

To let opportunities pass you by is to invite defeat, but to learn how to wait for a good opportunity and then to recognize it when it is right in front of you is the most basic element of success. And seizing your opportunities with determination and aggressiveness is the way to win all your ballgames and to win at life itself.

That is why this time around I hope you win. This time around, I hope you hit the shot. But to a great extent, your success or failure will depend on your timing. So you need to be smart and to know your opposition. You need to be perceptive and to understand the challenges ahead of you. To fully perceive the situation that awaits you and to grasp the realities of your surrounding circumstances is half the battle. But to know when to hold 'em and know when to fold 'em is the other half.

CONTROL

We are what we repeatedly do.
—Aristotle

C ARON BUTLER is a small forward for the Detroit Pistons and an established star in the NBA. But, like many of his contemporaries, Caron got off to a shaky start in life, and his road to success was a difficult one. Growing up on the streets of Racine, Wisconsin, Caron was a drug dealer by the time he was eleven, and he had been arrested fifteen times before he was fifteen years old.

"My role models back then were pimps (and) drug dealers," Caron told Oprah Winfrey in a 2005 interview. But it was during a stay in a maximum-security detention center that Caron discovered his passion in life. He realized that he had an amazing talent for basketball, and that newfound passion became the catalyst that inspired Caron to turn his life around.

Caron's real "pivot point" occurred when he was placed in solitary confinement for two weeks. "I remember writing my mother letters, so many letters," he said, "telling her how much I loved her and if I was to get out, I would never, ever hurt her again. It was from this moment I knew that I could do anything in life." Then, in time, Caron did get out of prison, and he never forgot the promise he had made to his mother.

So after finally obtaining the freedom he so desperately wanted, Caron took some big steps toward his goal of a better life. He went back to high school to get his diploma; then he joined the school's basketball team. And Caron's achievements in the classroom and on the court were so impressive, he eventually landed a full scholarship to play basketball for the University of Connecticut, where he led this high-profile team in both scoring and rebounding to become a second-team All-American. Then in 2002, following his sophomore year, Caron declared for the NBA draft and became the tenth overall pick, quite a leap from the desperate situation he had faced just seven years earlier.

But Caron was able to take a second shot at life by discovering his latent skills and by learning to utilize those skills for a noble purpose. He was able to take another shot because he bought into a God-given passion that gave him a much-needed focus for his talents and energy. And Caron was able to make this impressive turnaround by reaching a watershed moment where he firmly decided to take control of his future and to assume responsibility for his own destiny. Unlike so many of the young men around him, he became unwilling to let his circumstances dictate his outcome. Caron wanted to take hold of the wheel of his own life and guide the ship of his own providence. And that is precisely what he did.

So Caron learned what a lot of people just don't understand. Caron learned that, in both basketball and life, control is an essential element of success. In life, control over oneself is extremely important, and control over the elements of life that a person can rightly expect to influence is a prerequisite for success. On the basketball court, too, control is absolutely essential. In fact, a player cannot hope to score consistently unless he has control of the ball. And a player cannot hope to maintain control of the basketball unless he has control of his own body and control of the situation.

In the same way a golfer must manipulate the golf club so he can control the distance and trajectory of his shots and place the ball exactly where he wants it to go, a basketball player must be able to control his own body and control the basketball and the action on the court in order to consistently score against the opposing team. In basketball, a player must control his feet, control his hands, control his balance, and control his dribble while he is in possession of the ball. He must control his jump before he shoots, control his landing after he shoots, and control the release of the ball at the top of his jump. Players almost never score when they are out of control, and teams certainly must maintain control of themselves and of the game in order to win consistently.

In addition, players must be in control of their emotions, referees must be in control of the game, and coaches must be in control of their teams for the game of basketball to work and for an environment to exist where great players can do great things. In recent years, we have even come to realize that the authorities must maintain control of the crowds, because anything or anyone who is out of control can interfere with the game or even lead to the cancellation of a game. The same thing is true in life. Unless we maintain control of those things under our venue and authority, we can penalize ourselves very quickly and hinder our ability to make the shots we attempt.

Obviously, some things are beyond our control. For instance, a basketball player can't control the rules. He can't control the other team. He can't control the time clock or the referees or even the noise of the crowd. When these factors seem out of control, all he can do is maintain control of himself by first managing his emotions and then utilizing his training to manage his skills and to dictate the execution of his own game. But as a player manages himself and as a coach manages his team, the tide of a game can turn, just as life can slowly turn when we maintain control of ourselves and do the right things in the right way on a consistent basis.

We need only look at today's headlines to see the sad end that is the destiny of the person who is unable to control himself. In recent years, how many promising politicians have lost their careers in public service because they could not control their own conduct? And how many world-class athletes have lost their privileges to compete in the sports they love because they could not control their infatuation with gambling, drugs, or violence? How many great actors and entertainers have died in the prime of life because they could not say "no" to their own desires? Far too many promising people have squandered their God-given talents and opportunities by simply refusing to place reasonable restraints on themselves and their own behaviors.

Excellence brings great rewards, but excellence also requires great sacrifice. A talented athlete who would stay at the top of his game must go to bed early, condition himself daily, avoid the foods that aren't appropriate for him, and keep a safe distance from those who would use him or try to capitalize on his fortune. An accomplished athlete must learn to say "no" to himself when all the people around him are tripping over themselves to be his "yes" men.

If you have failed in the past, how much did your own lack of self-control contribute to your demise? Too many businessmen have bitten the dust because they wanted to go too far, too fast. Too many Realtors and mortgage brokers have lost their licenses because they could not stay within the boundaries of the law or the ethical standards that govern their chosen professions. Too many teachers have squandered their careers by getting too familiar with the minors they teach. Too many investors have rolled the dice, hoping for the big deal, only to lose everything on a foolish hunch.

If you can't control yourself, you can't win at the game of life. You must control your anger. You must control your impatience. You must control your need to prove yourself to others. You must control your anxiety about the future. You must control your regrets about the past. And every entrepreneur knows that the two emotions which destroy the greatest majority of their counterparts are the emotions of fear and greed. You must quickly learn to control these destructive forces in your life if you intend to complete your journey to success.

In *The Guardian,* a respected British newspaper, former President Bill Clinton explained in a 2004 interview how he had relied upon the advice of Nelson Mandela, the revered president of South Africa, to get him through a particularly difficult time in his presidency. In the interview, Clinton explained how he had visited Robben Island with President Mandela in 1998 to see the cell where Mandela spent 18 of his 27 years of imprisonment. And during that tour, Mandela gave Clinton the wisdom and encouragement that enabled the American president to move forward.

"(Mandela) told me he forgave his oppressors because if he didn't they would have destroyed him" Clinton explained. "He said: 'You know, they already took everything. They took the best years of my life; I didn't get to see my children grow up. They destroyed my marriage. They abused me physically and mentally. They could take everything except my mind and heart. Those things I would have to give away, and I decided not to give them away.' And then he said, 'Neither should you.'"

So being in control of yourself is the single most important factor in overcoming your challenges. It is the single most important factor in your success. No matter how talented you may be, how many opportunities you may have, or how perfect the timing may be for your big step forward, unless you can control your own actions and reactions, your mind and your emotions, your character and your will, you will not have a life of success. *You* are in control of you. You may not be in control of the circumstances around you, but you *are* in control of you. Don't give up that control.

One of the most famous prayers ever penned is the well-known "Prayer of Serenity" by Reinhold Niebuhr (1892–1971). Niebuhr wrote, "God, grant me the serenity to accept the things I cannot change; courage to change the things I can; and wisdom to know the difference." So the beginning of wisdom is to understand the difference between those things in your life that you *can* control and those things you *can't* control and then to respond accordingly. In fact, your recovery from past failures and your future ascent to greatness will begin and end with your ability to understand the distinction between those things that are under your control and those things that are beyond your control. But just as Niebuhr realized, you must do more than simply understand this difference; you must respond to your new understanding by gathering the courage that is necessary to turn loose of those things that are none of your business so you can more forcefully engage those things that should be the focus of your concern.

Denis Waitley, a founding member of the National Council for Self-Esteem, said, "Learn from the past, set vivid, detailed goals for the future, and live in the only moment of time over which you have any control: now." So as you prepare to get back on your feet and to make another effort to regain control of your life, ask yourself some honest questions about the task that lies ahead of you. Figure out what you can do to strengthen your chances for success at the same time you give consideration to those forces of life and nature that are actually beyond your control. You must make an informed and prudent decision whether or not this is the time to take another shot at your goals.

But if, after contemplating your options, you reach the conclusion that the potential rewards are worth the risks and that the time is right to move forward, go into your venture with your eyes wide open. Be prepared to deal with the inevitable problems that will flow from those parts of the equation that are beyond your reach and influence. And then take ownership of the decision you make. Store away the resources you will need to weather the inevitable storms, surround yourself with people who can bolster your chances for success, and draw up a game plan for the course you intend to walk. Take control of what you can. But be prepared simply to "stand" when the unexpected or the uncontrollable occur.

As Albert Ellis, a noted psychologist of the 1950s and one of the originators of cognitive-behavioral therapy, once said, "The best years of your life are the ones in which you decide your problems are your own. You do not blame them on your mother, the ecology, or the president. You realize that you control your own destiny."

Far too many people fail at what they attempt to do because they simply "roll the dice" instead of analyzing the challenge. They leave things to "fate" instead of taking control of their own fortunes. Obviously, it is unwise and irresponsible to try to manipulate things you can't sway. Life can quickly break the man who thinks he can control every facet of his environment. But few people fall short of their goals because they try to do too much; most people fail in their early attempts at great things because they don't take enough control of the elements they *can* affect. They don't "own" the things that are rightly their responsibility and legitimately their concern. However, the man who *does* take ownership of himself and his challenges, who accepts the realities that confront him, and who controls those things that are within the scope of his influence is the man who is traveling the road to success.

So how do we maintain control of this human tendency to either do too much or too little? How do we keep the desire for more in check while sustaining the motivation to do what we need to do? How can we keep fear and anxiety at bay while capitalizing on the drive and motivation in our hearts? The legendary story of US Airways pilot "Sully" Sullenberger can help us resolve this issue quite clearly.

On January 15, 2009, Sullenberger was captain of US Airways Flight 1549 from New York to Charlotte, North Carolina. But three minutes after the flight left LaGuardia Airport, the plane struck a flock of birds, causing both engines to fail. Captain Sullenberger assessed the situation and determined that neither returning to LaGuardia nor landing at another nearby airport was feasible. So as the flight crew prepared to ditch the plane in the Hudson River, Sullenberger told the passengers to "brace for impact." And in what became known as the "Miracle on the Hudson," Sully Sullenberger piloted the Airbus A320 to a safe water landing on the Hudson River, with no loss of life on the ground or among the 155 passengers and crew members aboard the aircraft.

Many people have praised Captain Sullenberger for his composure and calmness in this crisis situation. So during an interview with news anchor Katie Couric, Sullenberger explained his view on self-control. He said, "One way of looking at this might be that, for 42 years, I've been making small, regular deposits in this bank of experience, education, and training." And on January 15, the balance was sufficient so that I could make a very large withdrawal."

If you want to maintain control over your life in times of crisis, work toward that same goal every day. Make frequent deposits into your life bank of attitude, of effort, and of technique so you will be able to make a withdrawal when you are finally ready to take another shot at your dreams. And learn to appreciate and hone the various qualities you will need in order to succeed your next time around. Learn to say to yourself the things you need to believe and the things you need to do in order to fulfill your pursuits:

Rebounding — I will not consider a missed shot to be my final effort. I will try again.

Determination — I will be a person of steadfast resolve. I will not give up.

Aggressiveness — I will take the initiative, and I will work diligently.

Fearlessness — I will not let fear defeat me. I will face my fear and get in the game.

Preparation — I must learn and I must practice, putting my knowledge to work.

Positioning — I will place myself in a position to increase my chances for success.

Teamwork — We need each other. I can never do as much alone as I can do with a team.

Strength — I will have strength of purpose, endurance, and performance.

Balance — I will be aware of what is important in my life and juggle my responsibilities without dropping any balls.

Contact — Life is a contact sport. My conflicts will make me better, not bitter.

Timing — Everything in my life is a matter of timing. Good timing is essential to my success.

Control — To have control over myself and to create the best possible conditions for my next shot, I must passionately pursue these twelve qualities for my life.

In the opening chapter, I said I wanted this to be your comeback book, and it can be. Because your previous failures and missed shots are in the past, today can be a fresh start for you. With twelve traits of winners to incorporate into your life, you now have the tools at your disposal to help you move forward and take your next shot at the things that matter most to you.

My advice, therefore, as you prepare to take this step of faith, is to use the coaching I have offered to you to make a new plan, to set your daily and long-term goals, to nurture the proper mindset you will need to flourish, to gather your team around you for the enterprise ahead, and to set yourself in a position to hit the shot and win the game. You have the God-given talents you will need to succeed, the passion you will need to be motivated and persistent, and the keys that will unlock all the doors of opportunity that will confront you along the way.

So as I conclude my remarks to you and leave you to all the possibilities that await you in the future, I do so with confidence that victory is within your grasp and that the ability to triumph is within your soul. And that makes me feel good about saying to you, "Go ahead. Take another shot. This time, the outcome will be different. And the rest of your life will be the best of your life."

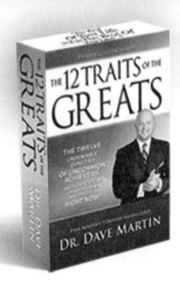

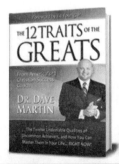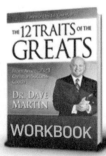

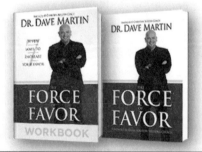